WHEN NOTHING IS IMPOSSIBLE

SPANISH SURGEON DIEGO GONZÁLEZ RIVAS' GLOBAL CRUSADE AGAINST CANCER AND PAIN

Elena Pita

Translation: Max Zalewski
(Fidelia Linguistic Solutions)
and Ngaire Blankenberg

ELENA PITA

WHEN NOTHING IS IMPOSSIBLE

SPANISH SURGEON DIEGO GONZÁLEZ RIVAS' GLOBAL CRUSADE AGAINST CANCER AND PAIN

bubok
EDITORIAL

Fundación
María José Jove

http://www.fundacionmariajosejove.org

© Elena Pita
© When Nothing Is Impossible

English edition: May 2018

Translation: Max Zalewski (Fidelia Linguistic Solutions) and Ngaire
Blankenberg
Cover: Iván Fandiño
Interior booklet photos: Daniel López – Mandeo Records
Author photo: © Rafa Jover
Back cover photo of the doctor and the author: Oscar Vales

ISBN paper: 978-84-685-2337-8
ISBN pdf: 978-84-685-2338-5

Legal deposit: M-19256-2018

Photographic composition: Bubok

To my son, Martín, so that you return.

Index

The fragrance of sandalwood and rosebay does not travel far.
But the fragrance of virtue rises to the heavens.
Dhammapada 4:11, sacred Buddhist text attributed
to Siddhartha Gautama, 6th Century BC

He rebelled not against the inevitability of death;
but that his robust and healthy organism
was fighting an insidious and cruel evil.
Giani Stuparich, *La isla*

PART ONE:
THE WAVE OF LIFE

CHAPTER 1:
Eighteen days adrift

*"Hello, I'm Diego. I'm going to do
my utmost to remove your tumor."*

That morning, she was scheduled to visit the hospital —
probably the place she loathed most. It was a hospital of
dirty walls, hallways overcrowded with ailing patients like
lifeless souls, and worn-down, burnt-out staff. She was there
to collect the results of the latest PET, a nuclear tomogra-
phy that evaluates tissue damage. Roughly two years ago,
Carmen López had been diagnosed with lung cancer. She
had wrested the last two years from life, as the tumor had
been discovered in a very advanced state (stage IV) and
had metastasized twice. But she never gave up. The love
and responsibility she felt towards her two young children
bolstered her with positive energy and strength, and she
responded excellently to the radiology and chemotherapy.
The treatments dissipated the dark spots that had spread to
her spinal column and esophagus, and decreased the main
tumor, which had been straining her vena cava. The results were so exceptional that the doctors went on to present them at medical symposiums. Carmen's strength was

impressive —for several months she was able to conceal the disease from the world, and even her elderly mother. She detested being pitied. During her private time, her hours of greatest loneliness, she would remember reading *The Etruscan Smile*. In this poignant novel, author José Luis Sampedro narrates the fight of an old partisan revolutionary farmer against his arch nemesis: la Rusca, a stomach cancer that would end up eating away at him until his final breath. Coincidentally, Sampedro had christened the disease with the same name as Carmen's mother's shepherd dogs; a name which had been passed down from one generation of dog to another.

There was no reason for that early December morning to be any different. On the wet streets under the cloud-blanketed sky, she arrived optimistically at the oncologist's office at the same foul hospital, expecting to hear what had already become routine: the original tumor had again reduced in size and activity, despite the new shadow that had alarmed doctors after the last X-ray.

"Carmen, it's growing back. That dark spot we saw is the tumor growing. It has spread aggressively, and it seems to have become immune to the chemo treatment. The gauges and markers are soaring. I talked with the surgeons and they still rule out the option of surgery." The words of her trusted oncologist left a dull, ringing sound in Carmen's ears. His words fell like an irrevocable and abrupt death sentence that she refused to accept.

Despite being numb from shock, she felt that within the doctor's words lay a tiny sliver of hope. Maybe her husband was hearing him more clearly. Dr. González was a young surgeon who had developed a minimally invasive technique using only a single incision and a camera. With this method, he had achieved many victories and dared to undertake the most bedeviling of thoracic tumors. Don't bother consulting anyone else, Diego will do this or nobody else in the world will.

"Go see him and do it now! Get going!" Doctor Fírvida was telling her as Carmen regained her hearing. "I immediately believed in it," she affirmed later. "He told me, 'If anyone can solve your disease, it's Diego. If there is any possibility of it happening, he's definitely the one.'"

***

Carmen's bed is being guided into the elevator on the way to the operating room. Barely 18 days have passed since her latest diagnosis. Eighteen nights of dread and panic, spent in her husband's arms, concealing any signs of the gravity of the situation from her two children and mother. Eighteen days and nights of steely mental control to avoid falling into despair.

As a child, Carmen suffered from polio during the final and fearsome plague of the virus that spread throughout Spain in the 1950's. Her first operation was at only 3 years old, when she was operated on by a German specialist in Madrid. He connected her tibia to her foot, which had become loose and dislocated. Later, at the age of 13, she underwent an experimental surgical technique by Doctor Esteve de Miguel, in which he used a z-shaped piece of metal to lengthen the tibias of 'the Polio children,' by two inches. Her father, a urologist, had not hesitated to entrust her to his Catalan colleague. In total, she had eight operations to stretch out the tibia. She suffered unspeakable pain and lost 25 pounds in 28 days. In the old Quirón Hospital in Barcelona, just the sight of Carmen made her mother exclaim to her husband, "I can't take any more suffering! Make it stop!" And her father, who would visit them on weekends, would tell the girl, "You have to endure." It was a devastating memory that would teach Carmen "to be tough and cold with myself for life."

"No. Of course I didn't accept the diagnosis (of the oncologist). He was telling me that any further efforts would no longer work, and that the strength I had mustered against the tumor until now was falling like a house of cards. How was I going to accept that?"

And that's how it went: she waited for 18 days, confident that everything was going to get better. "I have two young children and a wonderful partner who supported me; I had to keep seeing my children grow. Also, I believed deeply in science and medicine." Those 18 days consisted of racing to compile test results and clinical records and trying to pin down that prodigious surgeon who curiously had an office in a public hospital just 105 miles from her city, despite constantly traveling around the globe teaching his innovative technique.

The young surgeon, who after receiving the images of the tumor —God bless him— had said that yes, he'd operate. This, despite the fact that his own team had refused because they simply didn´t feel capable of handling her case: a mass located on the lung hilum, the central cavity between both lungs, where the heart veins begin, passing through the main thoracic arteries. The tumor measured 14 centimeters in diameter, invaded the upper right lobe, and was literally encrusted on the vena cava. On top of that, for two years, she had undergone intense radiology and chemotherapy, which had had debilitating consequences on her tissues. The diagnosis from the surgeons at her public hospital were definite, and grew even more so, "It's impossible. It's absolutely impossible to operate on you." But Carmen and her husband managed to speak with Diego and sent him the clinical records and the latest tests. Carmen's husband, the stomatologist, Ignacio Romero, will never be able to forget when the surgeon responded, "Impossible is nothing. I'll operate on her."

Diego clearly explained to Carmen's husband and brother-in-law (both doctors) the risks of the operation, which were plentiful, but that he, as a surgeon, and she, as a patient would be willing to take. "I was absolutely sure that I would take the risk," Carmen recounted months later. "It was the only hope possible. The treatments, besides already having been proven ineffective, had poisoned me unbearably for so long (first the "horse" radiation, and then 36 chemical sessions that burned like tiny stabbing at the top of my stomach). I was so debilitated that walking ten feet to the bathroom was like walking 100 miles."

It also didn't seem to them to be incredible, storybook-like, coincidental or outlandish that the surgeon had his office so close to A Coruña, "When they found the tumor in me," Carmen continued, "My husband contacted the entire world. We reached the conclusion that we had the best oncological medicine in Galicia, that my team in Ourense was (is) unbeatable, and that we wouldn't turn back. After undergoing treatment for one year, however, I did need a second opinion."

She told the lead oncologist on the team, and Doctor Fírvida agreed that yes, it's a good idea to have a second opinion. So, Carmen took her clinical records to a team led by Doctor Josep Baselga, who went on to become the

Medical Director of Memorial Sloan Kettering Cancer Center in New York, the most prestigious oncological center in the world. This new medical team would be led by this distinguished Catalan doctor, who personally treats his patients. She scheduled an appointment with the head of the lung cancer program at his institute in Barcelona. After interminable tests, Doctor Felip (Doctor Baselga's colleague and also a dear acquaintance of Doctor Fírvida) concluded that her tumor was incompatible with the immunotherapeutic treatments usually given by the Baselga Institute. She advised her to cease all chemotherapy because it would destroy her. That was something that the patient again could not accept, "It was as if they were telling me to give up fighting. No, that'll never happen." Continue with the chemo until it proves ineffective.

***

General elections were being held in Spain, and again, if there is such a thing as fate, the surgeon would be voting back in the country in a period of, that's right, 18 days. Carmen even gave thanks to politics. There wouldn't be time for a consultation prior to the surgery, Diego barely ever saw his medical team. They didn't feel capable of performing the operation themselves but hadn't hesitated to send the tests to their colleague, who was spending his days between Shanghai and the United States. The team was used to him tackling challenges that for anyone else would be impossible: those doctors knew that 'impossible' was a word that Diego would not tolerate.

***

As they wheeled her bed into the elevator to go down to the operating room, a striking young man dressed in blue scrubs suddenly made an abrupt entrance. He was accompanied by his colleague (and now Head of Services) Mercedes de la Torre, who was wearing a woolen toque. The young man approached the bed, "Carmen, how are you? I'm Diego" (that's what he said). "Everything will be fine. You'll see. We're going to do everything possible to remove that tumor from you." He took her hand and squeezed it gently but firmly.

Months later, Carmen would admit that the surgeon's extreme youth, his casual behavior and his humility concerned her. "My goodness," she told herself, "Close your eyes, and let´s get on with it. I had been expecting —or my subconscious had been expecting— a figure like that of the German surgeon who operated on me for the first time in Madrid at the age of three. That was my memory." It was a memory that continued to haunt her even as a student of economics in Madrid. "I accompanied a friend to an appointment with his orthopedic surgeon. He had also suffered from polio as a child, and that brought us together. When the doctor passed in front of me, I fainted. At the time, I didn't know why I had that reaction until I woke up and realized that it was the same German surgeon." She also had the image of the Catalan Doctor Esteve de Miguel etched in stone in her mind: his smile was 'slightly Machiavellian' when he exchanged information with her father, from surgeon to surgeon. Also unforgettable was her father's best friend: the feared pediatrician, with that low gravelly voice, always dragging deeply from his tobacco pipe, and clinking the little glass vials in his zinc box. "The image of Diego broke the standard of savior that I had had (or that

21

had been stored in my subconscious). And yes, perhaps it made me harbor a few doubts; as I was waiting to be let into the operating room, all these thoughts crossed my mind." She closed her eyes and got on with it.

CHAPTER 2:
A Crusade Against Fear and Pain

"One who has not gone through it cannot begin to imagine
what a person feels when they hear these words:
'You have cancer.'"

"Why even dare to try, doctor?"

"It's a matter of experience: I feel capable because I believe that with the practice I've had, I can handle the complex cases."

'Super complex' are the words he uses to describe the terminal cases he sees so frequently. Only yesterday he had operated on one of these 'super complex cases' in the Rambam Medical Center, Haifa; the previous week it was an illustrious citizen of the United Arab Emirates, who had traveled to be operated on during a course he was giving in Amman, Jordan. Diego González Rivas (A Coruña, August 12, 1974) does not like to say he's courageous, instead he prefers to point to his experience. At 42, his surgical statistical record undoubtedly shatters all others. Still, he's not one to gather statistics like trophies, even though in 2015 alone, he performed more than 800 major surgeries at Shanghai Pulmonary Hospital. It is the largest center for pulmonary medicine in the world, and in addition to regularly working there, he also directs an international training seminar there every two months. Eight hundred major surgeries when the great thoracic surgeons (in a country like Spain) average less than 10% of that, meaning they perform no more than two or three surgeries per week, often only one.

"Doesn't it scare you to be responsible for such astounding figures, and the many lives stretched out on operating tables hoping that your hands will restore their ability to live?"

"You are so overtaken by the technical side that you stop thinking about the person and the feelings they expressed days earlier in the consultation, because that would debilitate you. There is a tumor in front of you and nothing else. The patient doesn't exist, it is sterile, with neither history nor life. I think I would even be perfectly capable of operating on my father with the same detachment and resolve. Logically, it's something you acquire with experience. I enter the surgery room and I transform: I concentrate on the tumor, the patient is now anonymous, a barcode, a number. You only go back to seeing their human dimension when the surgery ends. The worst thing that can happen in a surgery room is panic; if you start to panic, you're lost, and if feelings are caught in the middle, panic spreads much more easily."

***

Part of the blame is due to pain —his aversion to others' pain— and another part is due to laughter —his desire to spread happiness. As a child, he grew up believing in making possible the most difficult task: the joy of others.

Armed with a cassette player, holed up in his room, he'd record tapes of jokes so that he could crack a smile on the faces of whoever listened to them. He dreamed of being an entertainer, a comedian in the literal sense of the word. When he saw gloomy elderly people, he swore that he'd cure their pain someday. That's how those who knew him best remember him. The second part (the curing) ended up being more urgent than bringing laughter, and that's why he's a surgeon. As a result, his life is a total commitment, traveling around the world, practicing and teaching his revolutionary technique: Uniportal VATS. Using this method, a surgeon can remove the most lethal lung cancer through a small intercostal port, only occasionally requiring sedation and local anesthesia. After a painless post-operation period, the patient is sent home 48 hours after the surgery.

Diego's mother, his guiding light and emotional support, works as a postpartum nurse in the city's Public Maternity Hospital. Nobody was surprised when her teenager chose his path. He who had been the leader of a group of gypsy boys in the neighborhood next to his grandparents' house; who had distracted the class at every opportunity; who had bungee jumped using climbing ropes, even though he had never seen it done before; who had surfed waves of the most turbulent coasts, ultimately, opted to study medicine.

Although he trained in thoracic surgery, he would not be immune to the pain and suffering of his patients: the torture of slitting the chest and forcing the thoracic cavity open with the rib retractor. It was an assault that oncological patients rarely survived. He dedicated his life to a crusade of saving lung patients from an agony that he also could not bear. He invented and perfected a minimally invasive and painless technique to remove tumors and operate on severe conditions of the thoracic cavity. Now he travels around the entire world disseminating and teaching it; in this way, he has been able to give relief and joy to thousands of patients and their loved ones, waiting for the five prescribed years to pass before proclaiming the cancer has been cured.

***

He communicates with his patients and surgeons from all over the world through Facebook (his page has already reached its 5,000-follower limit). He is also the world pioneer of broadcasting medical advances on social media. He opened the first surgery channel on YouTube, diegogonzalezrivas surgery channel; more than 2,000 surgeon subscribers follow him. Every time he uploads or posts something, the news is shared instantly 500, 1,000, 2,000 times.

He has come to A Coruña on just a three-day break between Strasbourg, where he gave a course on Uniportal VATS, and Havana, where he will do a live surgery for Fidel Castro's medical team. There, he will also receive a tribute from the top brass of the government and their favored artists. That's how they thank Diego around the world: he teaches, and governments and medical administrations of the large hospitals honor him for his efforts. He dedicates almost all of his time to operations and courses for which he does not charge (except for those organized by companies that manufacture surgical equipment). To do this, he takes unpaid leave from his work as a doctor at Sergas (*Servizo Galego de Saúde*).

He awakens early in his home. It is a house in one of the modern and impersonal sub-divisions of the city. The first order of the day is to head to the coast to scan the waves. Today, the wind is blowing from the northwest, which churns the sea: impossible to surf. Instead, he goes with a friend to swim in one of the municipality's Olympic swimming pools, the San Diego Pool near the port. In front of the sea, his sea, he speaks enthusiastically about his childhood and career. We are in Riazor Beach, where he grew up, under a rainy, gray sky that from time to time allowed the timid winter sun to shine through. Later, he will eat with his whole family who are waiting for him with great excitement: two months without seeing him.

Also waiting for him tomorrow (Monday) are two emergency patients who have come to the small Galician town: one from Riyadh, Saudi Arabia, and the other from San José, Costa Rica. The first patient was sent to Diego by his oncologist in Saudi Arabia, who believes the patient is a case for surgery, but only trusts Diego. The second patient is an elderly woman (above 80), who only her North American oncologist and Diego deemed suitable for operation. Both will be successfully operated on in the Saint Raphael Surgery Institute of A Coruña (one of the centers in which his Minimally Invasive Thoracic Surgery Unit operates), next to the Juan Canalejo University Hospital Complex (CHUAC), where Diego is an attending physician in the Public Health Department.

Sitting next to the turbulent ocean that day in Riazor, Diego talks about his patients. Everything starts with a verdict: 'You have cancer.' "Nobody can imagine what a person feels when they hear that sentence. Fear takes over, and suddenly, your insides burn. You feel like you're constantly swimming against the tide, and that white-hot fear resurfaces again and again, you trust desperately that the science of medicine will be your salvation." Until you're cured, or until a second verdict confirms the worst-case scenario, that of the abyss, *there's nothing else that can be done.*

That's what happened to Carmen, Hadid, Joaquín, and the majority of his patients. Remember that in 2015 alone, he performed 800 major surgeries, many of them very complex cases, which occasionally had metastasized, and were treated with intensive radiography and chemotherapy while still effective. Stubborn and shocking cases, stage IV, misery. Many of Doctor Diego González's patients have heard the sentence, "There's nothing left that can be done," and they sleep with that inside, and wake up, and go back to sleep, until he places himself like a firewall between the verdict and the clinical case.

"We're surgeons. Surgical patients reach us, and that's just 20% of all patients. When the disease has spread to other areas, our capacity to act is very limited and operating is not recommended. But each patient must be treated as an individual, and in the remaining 80%, cases are selected based on their responses to treatment and their tumor's behavior. Even in advanced stages, they can receive what we call a 'rescue surgery.' There is hope for those patients despite the complexity, as long as we have the support or authorization of the oncologist." In the aforementioned cases of the Saudi Arabian and Costa Rican patients, the oncologist had not said "it's a case for surgery," rather "let's talk to Diego."

"They are very technically complex cases that only expert hands can operate on, assuming the very real risks of an accident in the surgery, or of an adjacent tissue being torn or scratched, likely the vena cava and the heart." The surgeon's deepest fear is of a hemorrhage (bleeding in organs or tissues like the brain or vena cava) that may be fatal within instants if it is not addressed in time. In addition, gushing blood taints one's vision, even more so when seeing an image through a camera, which must be constantly washed during the operation. "There is always a major risk for the patient when the location and history of the tumor are so complex. But in our unit (in his hands), these risks are minimized because of our experience. I've been through some really difficult situations in all types of countries and conditions, by myself, without my instruments or my team, in tremendously complex cases. When you overcome one challenge like that, your skills multiply."

So, he does dare. "I don't like to say that I dare to try; rather that I feel qualified because of my experience, and I believe in what I can do." He is only 42 years of age, with just 13 years in the surgery room as an assisting physician and world traveler. But, Dr. González Rivas doesn't care about figures or calculations. Decked out in an (immaculate) surfer shirt and skinny jeans, underneath his parka with a fur hood, without a hint of arrogance on his baby face, he says, "It's impossible for me to calculate a total number of operations I've done, although most probably, I'm one of the surgeons who's done the most lung tumor operations in the world."

CHAPTER 3:
I'll Perform Your Operation

The extreme situations I've experienced have led me to do things that in theory you'd think belong to the universe of magic. In the end, you realize the human being is exceptional.

You have cancer. There is nothing left to do. An alien has taken over your body and is growing as fast as you are dying; strangling your viscera, intoxicating your cells, traveling at will through your blood until it lethally obliterates you.

There is no effective nor palliative care to soothe oncological patients. They clamor for it to be removed or vomit it out if possible. Doctor, get this out of me, clean my body, find the closest sword, cure me.

It's either Diego or nobody. The trust becomes blind, it blinds them. "The patients end up being willing to have anything done to them, and the sooner the better. Everything you say is going to sound good to them. They end up blindly having trust in me because the reality is that they have no other choice: what I offer them will be their final option, and therefore, they are totally committed patients. Normally, the patient doesn't talk very much, but observes a lot of what I say or do; and they know everything about me. Maybe they haven't read anything personally, but their family has, and has told them about me: I become their hope. I obviously feel a great responsibility because of their decision. Balancing what I can do, what I think can be done and what I'm going to do becomes a sort of personal challenge. For those things, I have confidence in myself; I assume regularly that my opinion will be contrary to other surgeons who have previously evaluated them. I'm not a lunatic or irresponsible person (he doesn't even consider himself brave). I go about it that way because I have confidence in my vast experience. Having operated in so many places around the world, without a team, in hospitals without instruments or equipment, very complicated cases, situations that have made me suffer and sweat. All that makes you tough and you discover some personal resources that you had never imagined. I imagine that it's due to humans' survival instinct. It's an adaptation to the environment; until you experience it, you consider it impossible. But it's like people who have their lives turned upside down by going blind, but then end up achieving things that they never would have fathomed before. The extreme situations that I've experienced have led me to do things that in theory you'd think would belong to the universe of magic. In the end, you realize that the human being is exceptional." Magic, like the impossible, is nothing.

***

Earlier, we mentioned a moment during an appointment, when a patient who has been rejected by so many other surgeons hears that yes, he or she will be operated on. "The family member accompanying them is always the one who talks, and the patient is silent and observing, as though looking for signs. They are scared. They know the surgery you're going to practice on them is not easy, and it calms them down for me to downplay the matter and be warm, which is not difficult whatsoever for me, because that's how I am: I'm warm and caring. Standing up during the consultation, shaking the patient's hand, exchanging two kisses on the cheek —that all comes from within. It calms them down, and suddenly I become a trusted support. All of that relieves them, because they see a way out, a possibility. It even shows on their faces. They lose the guarded expression they entered with. I consider it an essential part of my job, like visiting them in the room when I have finished the surgery, talking with them, taking them by the hand and giving them a kiss. It generates empathy that works very well with the patient. It's fundamental for their emotional well-being. I am lucky that these things come very naturally to me, without being forced. That's how I am.

"When you treat this type of patient, it's very important to take into account what they're going through emotionally. A cancer patient is always going to interpret each one of your gestures and movements. Because they mistrust, they fear being deceived or that, in one way or another, you're holding information back from them, which occasionally the families do to protect them. So, the first thing I do is to look them in the eyes and explain to them very directly and clearly what the situation is. Although later they interpret gestures and words in a way you'd never suspect." Perhaps because of this, Diego scrutinizes others through his near-sighted eyes: look forward, fixate on the eyes through dark thick glasses, perched under his black thick eyebrows. And what do you tell them? "There's always hope for my patients. I look for the right explanation, without ever deceiving them, always measuring my words. Because a patient without hope dies, you kill them. We know from statistics that a stage IV oncological patient has a very low survival rate, and within five years, the tumor tends to recur. So yes, in general, it is very difficult to cure them, but there are select cases that are outside the norm, and who is to know which patient is within that small percentage that will be cured? In reality one never knows how each patient is going to react. Therefore, I opt for hope, for keeping them up to date on new drugs or the possible healing effects of surgery, but without ever hiding the truth. And in the 20% of operable cases, assuming the inherent risk of a complicated surgery, I'm confident I can save them."

Every time Doctor González goes back to this fateful statistic, he insists on the importance of preventative medicine in cases of a history of lung cancer. Screening, CAT scans and periodic low resolution/radiation scans are crucial in order to be able to detect a virulent tumor. In 80% of cases, the tumor is discovered in non-operable stages because it doesn't cause symptoms and usually occurs in smokers who already have pulmonary disorders, like chronic coughing, respiratory insufficiency and other anomalies. It's nothing new for them —a discomfort they've already incorporated into their normal day. He believes that the future is in screening, something that is already practiced in the United States, for example. It's done so that the small node that starts as the tumor can be removed in time, before invading the blood veins that surround it and spread around scot-free. "80% of non-operable tumors probably were operable at the start but were not detected in time. That's the key."

***

Uniportal VATS (Video-Assisted Thoracic Surgery) — the curative and painless technique invented by Dr. Diego González Rivas.

Carmen has left the operating room. It has been four hours of surgery, with no option other than applying general anesthesia and putting a tube in her —such was the degree of complication of the expected surgery. The tumor was located in the lung hilum, and in contact with the mediastinum (the cavity that separates both lungs, and contains the heart, the large blood vessels, trachea, thymus and connective tissues). Because she had previously undergone radical chemo-radiation treatment, hers was a case that was "very complex, very difficult, technically speaking." It's difficult to remove the tumor entirely and is at a high risk due to its proximity to the vena cava (if it tears it will result in the feared hemorrhage). This meant the possibility of a vascular reconstruction had to be factored in, which was a path few were willing to travel. "It was a pain," the doctor admitted, blushing slightly because of his word choice and the sincerity of his expression. But the tumor had been encapsulated in such a way that it became one of those cases that Diego called 'selected,' due to the excellent or practically prodigious response to the treatment. It was an operable case and he had assumed the risk.

***

In the recovery room, they give her the news. "Carmen, everything went really well. The surgery was successful," her husband says into her ear. Carmen could barely register his words, but she did feel him: she felt her husband's immense smile, radiating through him —the smile and happiness emanating from him, that she did register. Dr. González had been able to remove all of the tumor through a very small incision between the chest and the right dorsal. But Carmen had dozed off, still under the fumes of the anesthesia, painless. She wouldn't feel it when her nerve endings and conscience fully woke up.

Less than 12 hours later, she was moved from the recovery room to her own room, where visiting family members began to trickle in, unstoppable against such extraordinary and unexpected, practically incredible news. Carmen was breathing well, with a perfect recovery from the first instant. That same afternoon her sister found her sitting in the little chair next to the bed, drinking a latte, which another sister had brought up from the cafeteria —comings and goings. She didn't feel pain, just a little discomfort around the small incision and its suture, and everything suddenly started to seem like a miracle. The text messages began to fly. Everyone was preparing to celebrate the next day, December 24. Carmen, however, had to stay in hospital in bed, and could not attend the grand Christmas Eve dinner, a big disappointment to her loved ones.

At six that evening, Diego entered her room at San Rafael Hospital, "Carmen, how are you?"

"Well, pretty good actually, not even a little pain or discomfort."

"I'm going to remove the drainage catheter" (directly to the lung, inserted through the one and only incision). "Lie down." He removed it. "How's that?"

"Good."

"Great, then get dressed. You're going home to celebrate Christmas Eve."

***

Less than 48 hours had passed since leaving the surgery room. Carmen could barely believe it as she passed through the hospital doors. It was cold and raining hard. La Rusca remained silent in a formalin bottle, sealed for anatomical pathology.

Nobody in her family could believe what had happened either. After living two years — exactly 24 months— of shared anguish, clinging to a blind hope, a surgeon from their own city had made the dream come true, extracting a cancer from her when it had been declared a short-term terminal case that no surgeon considered operable. That time had been so long, dense, painful and sad...especially given their family history. Carmen's father had died around 25 years earlier, young and strong, due to a lethal tumor on his pancreas that spread to his liver without any doctor having been aware of the disease until its final stage. He died in the family home, surrounded by his loved ones, profoundly sedated because he could never accept his own death. "Bring me the best surgeon to get this out of me!" he desperately barked to his son, also a doctor. There were a total of six doctors in the family; but there was nothing left to do, and the father, at 67 years of age, who seemed to be unbeatable, such was his fortitude and brilliance, died in silence, in a single sigh, within the short period of six weeks after being diagnosed. Just nine years ago, her brother had left them as well, in one breath his soul escaping through the window in the room where Carmen had left him to die, surrounded by the family. Her older brother was an urologist like their father (from the Catalan school of the prestigious Dr. Antoni Puigvert). Although his own team was able to remove their brother's first kidney tumor; the same could not be repeated when the evil cells reemerged in the pancreas and liver. A terrible memory and outcome that had come back to her, as she sat in the same place, that mansion atop the cliff of the Ares estuary. Undeniably, it was a miracle.

Her happy mother would only find out about Carmen's disease just a few months after the 'surgical rescue.' That Christmas Eve, she ate supper by her daughter's side. Carmen took the place of the deceased older brother at the large family table that her mother presided over every Christmas in front of the children, grandchildren and great-grandchildren. She didn't perceive anything unusual in the great joy of the others, as they celebrated life. They had told her that Carmen had been operated on for a cyst in her lung, and that's why her hands were inflamed from the intravenous pathways and her face was set in an expression of both incredulity and fear.

Note: Carmen can no longer bear to eat monkfish, because the meat of the fish is so similar to the consistency of her lung tumor whose images she had seen in the videos that Dr. González disseminates around the world on social media.

**

Normally, the person who enters the recovery room gives the news, and the patient, still drowsy or doped up on anesthesia, smiles back. The next day, their faces become transformed with joy: now conscious, they've heard the doctor's prognosis from the surgery through the family. "Of course, in addition you also feel good and without pain. Without knowing what happened inside the operating room, your optimism is accentuated by your feeling of well-being. When you are in pain, it's difficult to appreciate good news or externalize joy, because the pain paralyzes you; with pain, I wouldn't even be able to trust that the result was good. The next day, I find most patients already sitting up, and when I explain the results, their joy is immense."

"Is it always that way, doctor?"

"The most complicated part is making the decision about whether or not to operate on patients that have barely any pulmonary function or very limited cardiac reserves. You know that surgery can be curative, and the rest is generally just palliative, but the act of operating may complicate the situation if there are post-operative difficulties. There's a very low probability, but it exists. If the patient has even the most minimal infection, there can be a snowball effect, which can result in death. You're aware of the risk, and in front of you, you have a person, who despite having a tumor in their lung, appears to be fine and has a normal life. Yes, it's happened a few times, complications that after two or three days in chronic pulmonary patients, become uncontrollable and the patient passes away." Medicine will never be an exact science, nor will the surgeon.

"Also, sometimes enormously difficult surgical situations arise that make you suffer. This occurred to me especially during my first travels, me by myself around the world. For example, I remember a patient in Saudi Arabia. It was an extremely complicated case: a very obese man with a central tumor that required a very complex reconstruction. My assistants didn't have any experience in video-assisted surgery and we were operating live in a large auditorium. It was a very tense surgery, but in those moments,

I concentrate so that the tension doesn't paralyze me. It's like I'm in another state of being. I'm not afraid and I can proceed to make the necessary decisions.

"I remember another patient in Jerusalem, whom I operated on with another inexperienced assistant. It was a bilobectomy (the removal of both lobes of the same lung). The man had an anatomical anomaly that had not been detected and started to bleed. Those were moments of great tension, because you have to decide —do I open him up or continue through the single incision? It was all happening in a surgery broadcast live to an auditorium."

***

The messages of thanks that he receives are indescribable, innumerable and even still, none is able to express more than a tiny part of the gratitude felt by the patients and family members. Like those extraordinary first-page ads in the local paper that more than once have surprised Dr. González's team, such as the following:

"*Thank you to the thoracic surgery specialists. Minimally Invasive Thoracic Surgery Unit. Dr. Diego González Rivas, Dr. Mercedes de la Torre, Dr. Ricardo Fernández Prado, for these new 7 years of quality living —your patient, Luis Alberto Calviño Suárez.*"

This morning, from Amman, where he teaches a course on Uniportal VATS to thoracic surgeons from Jordan and other neighboring countries, and where he had just completed a live surgery in front of his fellows (students in medical jargon), Diego sent a photo as a response to the question, "What message has made you the most excited during these years of touring and healing?"

It was left to him at the reception of his hotel in Amman, attached to an elegant box of chocolates, by the mother of the patient he had operated on live. The patient was a 50-year-old man, and he was a complex case (very similar to Carmen's, he pointed out), who had arrived from Dubai to be operated on (free of charge, for the good of science) as part of the course. Oncologists had recommended him for surgery, but none of the Arab and American surgeons consulted wanted to perform the operation. Diego did. The results were optimal, again a curative surgery. Later, Diego would find out that the man was the CEO of one of the major business corporations in the Emirates, and that his father holds the presidency of the highest court of justice in the country. A 'bombshell' patient."

"Dear Doctor,

It has been a pleasure to meet a surgeon of such genius. It will be our pleasure to receive you in the UAE (United Arab Emirates) whenever you desire. Thank you so much. We will continue to follow your enormous feats and achievements. God bless you." Signed, Hadid's mother.

The mother had seen all of the documentaries in which Diego explains his technique and his travels for healing. "I know about you," she told him in the post-operating room, as she kissed him in a frenzy of joy.

The messages are all similar. Nobody can express such gratitude: giving you back a life that yesterday you thought was lost.

CHAPTER 4:
Think Different, Dream, and Make It Possible

Why must the post-operation period be so difficult and painful for patients? We must 'think different' and use our imagination: why isn't it possible to alleviate it?

He was afraid of others' pain, he hated the patients' suffering. He said to himself: "We must think carefully and use our imagination, why is it not possible?" The axiom had originated with him, although he may not yet have known it. Use your imagination and you make it possible: you *can* save the lives of dozens of patients diagnosed with lung cancer who have been deemed *terminal* (he preferred to say, "rejected by conventional surgery") who probably wouldn't survive the aggressiveness of open surgery, the devastating attack on the eroded immune system, or who perhaps would have died, drowning from the pain.

"It's always possible to take the positive from the negative, you just need to see it differently. When I dream, or look to the future, I always have a positive attitude. Negativity comes easily, it doesn't make sense to nurture it by focusing on it. I think this is essential to being happy. A person creates the positive with their strength of character, their energy and their determination; the rest are just temporary obstacles, like an illness, professional jealousies and broken hearts."

Diego was speaking sitting in front of the ocean, and people would periodically approach to congratulate him. Already they knew about his achievements, about his international recognition. This week he had been selected as one of the 10 best Spanish doctors, chosen from amongst all specialties. Diego had begun to appear often on television and in the national press.

"And as for the obstacles, I take them as life lessons to improve and to grow; to not be over-confident or too comfortable. It's my philosophy of life: to learn from obstacles because they always happen for a reason: you've just got to know how to redirect negativity, to convert it into motivation. A life without obstacles is probably a life without success because you become over-confident, and excessive self-confidence makes one arrogant, or indifferent or too ambitious. You lose sight of what is truly important. You've got to know how to be prepared for the unpredictable, such as a lung tumor in a non-smoking person; but without dwelling on it, because you can invoke it. Today, I'm the happiest person in the world, but tomorrow I may have some really tough times. That's why it's important to enjoy every minute, to enjoy the now and to think positively." That is the philosophy that Diego has adopted through his own life experience, and what he has absorbed from the many cultures he has encountered throughout his tours. You might think he has been reading the principles of the Dharma, the Buddhist path to virtue, enlightenment, and therefore happiness. But he has come to his own conclusion, like Uniportal VATS: "Live your life positively."

That's essentially what Doctor Diego González said in the 18-minute Ted Talk he did in 2013, entitled 'The Pioneers' Journey'. Diego explained the connection between his childhood (because everything begins in childhood), the circumstances of his life and the Uniportal VATS technique that the surgeon today is spreading around the world to save lives. How dreaming the impossible has "made life better for many people," has reduced pain and suffering, and has given time back to patients, who, even though he doesn't like to say it, had been terminally ill or rejected by conventional surgery.

Exactly midway through the 18 minutes, Diego González cited the great visionary Steve Jobs to define people like them: "Here's to the crazy ones. The misfits. The rebels. The troublemakers. The round pegs in the square holes. The ones who see things differently. They're not fond of rules. And they have no respect for the status quo. You can quote them, disagree with them, glorify or vilify them. About the only thing you can't do is ignore them. Because they change things. They push the human race forward. And while some may see them as the crazy ones, we see genius. Because the people who are crazy enough to think they can change the world, are the ones who do." This is the text narrated in a 1997 Apple marketing campaign under the slogan *Think different.* In one version, Steve Jobs reads the text in the background while on screen appear the faces of Albert Einstein, Alfred Hitchcock, Maria Callas, Martin Luther King Jr., John Lennon, Mahatma Gandhi, Lloyd Wright, Pablo Picasso and many other revolutionaries.

"But 'thinking different' in the field of medicine can be very risky because it affects the human being's most valuable asset: their health," Diego cautioned in his Ted Talk, before going on to say, "Despite that, I always knew that I had to think differently: I'm a restless person and I like to innovate. Therefore, I had to learn to measure the risk." Such are the traits of a visionary.

***

"Is Dr. González a visionary?"

"In surgery, yes, I think I am; and also, in spreading it through social media. I think I have the ability to foresee where things will go (and then change them)."

The streets are filling with people, walking around in their winter coats, lured out by a timid sun, although still sprinkled with a few drops of rain. The congratulations from his hometown neighbors start to multiply. He thanks them, one by one, with a hug, kiss, smile, handshake and gentle words. He feels good in his city for a few hours, one or two days at most, then back to his sojourns abroad. Havana, Riyadh, Amman, Cairo, Jerusalem, Taiwan, Baltimore (7 cities in 7 days-also the name of the documentary about his work *7 days, 7 cities*), Tibet, China, Palestine, Slovenia, Japan and an etcetera that not even he knows when, how or where will find its final point.

In the shadow of that uncertain future, let's go back in time to search for some clarity. When and how did Doctor Diego González Rivas reach the conclusion that the form of operating on lung patients must change? He laid it out in an article published in the Journal of Thoracic Disease in August 2014. "When I started my work as a resident in the Thoracic Surgery Unit at the Juan Canalejo University Hospital in A Coruña in 1999, I wondered why the patient's post-operating period had to be so hard and painful, due to the enormous and traumatic incision and separation of the ribs? I couldn't stop turning the question over and over in my head, and this became a huge challenge for me: what could be done to reduce and facilitate a better quality of life for patients after the operation?"

In the words of Doctor César Bonome, an anesthesiologist at CHUAC and the Coordinator of Anesthesia, Recovery and Pain Treatment at San Rafael Hospital, the deep anesthesia alone that the open thoracotomy requires, increases the post-operative mortality and the potential of cognitive dysfunction. "There are even patients who, after an operation like that, never return to being the same. Why? Because anesthesia, when administered at such a high concentration, kills the neurons to a certain degree." Those are the words of a great expert in anesthesia, admired by the many patients who have been treated by his gentle hands.

There was no specific moment in his surgical experience that shaped him this way and set him on his crusade against pain; it has been more of a continuum, an intolerance of outside suffering that was born inside him, without him knowing it. However, Doctor González does have one memory from his trajectory, that perhaps was subconsciously instrumental.

"He was a young patient, 45 years old, on whom we had practiced a thoracotomy. We left a catheter in him for the epidural anesthesia, something we used to do to alleviate their pain as much as possible. The day after the operation, I was on-call at the hospital and they called me because the catheter had come loose, and he was dying of pain.

We administered intravenous and subcutaneous morphine, and other analgesics, but the man wouldn't stop screaming. He couldn't take the suffering. I was so overwhelmed, I spent the whole night going back to see him practically every two seconds. I remember his face, that expression of abject horror, and his words. He told me he was dying, and please do something, because he couldn't take it, and it was absolutely horrible.

"It's not that it was something new or unknown. He wasn't the first I had seen desperate and wanting to die or who felt like he was dying. It wasn't a unique experience, but I do remember then, that I was more aware than ever: it was necessary to do something to avoid that hell. The hell that a patient endures when, due to one factor or another, because the epidural doesn't function properly, or because he doesn't respond to the common analgesic, he needs to be administered morphine. In these situations, it is very complicated to control pain with morphine because it depresses the respiratory system and can cause a lack of oxygen. You need to find a balance in administering it. And no, in that case we weren't able to control it. The man spent the whole night writhing in pain, until he finally half slept due to the extremely high dose of analgesic. Again, he wasn't the only one. I remember many cases like him.

"A thoracotomy puts pressure on the nerves of the chest and back in such a way that sometimes the pain persists their entire lives. That's what we call post-operative neuralgia. Remember that the separation of the ribs sometimes exceeds 8 inches, depending on the volume of the surgery, meaning the size of the tumor."

***

Doctor Diego González chose two quotations to present in his article in the Journal of Thoracic Disease in August 2014, in which he recounts the long journey that spans from the open thoracotomy (traditional lung operation) to the Uniportal VATS or video-assisted surgery through a unique and minimal incision.

> *"Humans are allergic to change. They love to say, 'We've always done it this way.' I try to fight that. That's why I have a clock on my wall that runs counter-clockwise."*
> Grace Hooper (pioneer computer scientist)

> *"There's a way to do it better: Find it!"*
> Thomas Edison

"I started to study the origins of thoracoscopic surgery and was immediately fascinated. In 1910, the physician Hans Christian Jacobeus (Stockholm), described the first thoracoscopy to release adhesions in tuberculosis patients. Before him, in 1901, the German surgeon Georg Kelling had practiced it on dogs, but never published his results. Thus, Jacobeus is considered the father of the invention. For many decades, the procedure was relegated to diagnostic use and minor therapies. It wasn't until 1992 when the Italian professor Giancarlo Roviaro decided to practice the first pulmonary resection to surgically treat a cancer through small incisions, using a camera and screen, without splitting open the ribs. He made the highly important step that goes from a highly aggressive open surgery to a minimally invasive procedure, using just three small incisions, which allowed the patient a much better post-operative recovery. The discovery revolutionized thoracic surgery. As a result, he was criticized for many years by more traditional surgeons, those who considered themselves to be more prestigious and who proclaimed that the procedure was not appropriate for oncological surgery.

However, time would prove him right. His surgical praxis through small incisions showed that it was not only possible, but that his patients had much less pain, and their recovery was much faster. Nevertheless, the medical community refused to accept something that was obvious, and it was many years before this development was recognized.

After my research, I decided that I had to learn this technique. So I investigated which hospital had the most experience in video-assisted surgery in the whole world."

In 2007, Diego requested unpaid leave, and adding it to his unused vacation, he was able to finance a stay at Cedars Sinai Hospital of Los Angeles, where he learned the video-assisted technique through three or four incisions from the hands of the most experienced surgeons in the world, under the guidance of Doctor Robert McKenna. When he returned, he started to put it into practice in the thoracic unit of the A Coruña University Hospital. There, he began a fateful chapter of his life we'll discuss later, in the chapter titled "Obstacles."

***

"When, despite the obstacles, I was able to gain enough experience, I decided that I should improve the use of the technique or even try to improve the technique itself. So I moved back to the United States." This time, he felt (or his intuition told him) that the best opportunity would be at the Memorial Sloan Kettering Cancer Center in New York, probably the most renowned medical center for oncological treatment and research in the world. He wasn't wrong. Diego doesn't believe in destiny, but that 'everything happens for a reason.' Yet it is difficult for him to not use the term when he refers to the enormous luck that he found there. "By chance, I encountered a person who changed my way of thinking."

In the hallways of Memorial Hospital, he met a colleague who told him that in his hospital they had started to practice video-assisted surgery though two single incisions. It was Duke University Medical Center Hospital in North Carolina. "That left me really confused. I wasn't able to understand his verbal explanation. In my mind, at least three holes were essential: one to insert and handle the surgical material, another for the camera, and third incision to support the lung. I asked him to draw it on a piece of paper."

The rough sketch on paper would change his life and that of so many people around the world. Upon returning to Spain, the piece of paper became his obsession: he could not understand the technique depicted by those pen drawings. He decided to go to Duke and touch the Holy Grail with his own hands. He contacted the Head of Thoracic Surgery at the American center, who directly responded that he does not accept anybody in his department whom he doesn't know, not even as a visitor. However, Diego didn't settle for that answer. At this point in his life, or in his story, it is easy to imagine his reaction. He looked for the first presentation of that American Head of Thoracic Surgery at a conference and showed up as a spectator. "I went to the annual meeting of the American Thoracic Society, decided to meet Doctor D'Amico, and after an unforgettable conversation with him, I asked him to give me the opportunity to visit his institution, and that's how I was accepted. Thanks to my persistence, today Doctor D'Amico and I are great friends, and we organize courses together. Thanks to my persistence in pursuing an idea. If I hadn't believed in it, I would have never met him, and I wouldn't be showing others how I did it either."

He returned from his apprenticeship in North Carolina, and that is when the "Obstacles" chapter acquired a capital "O." For the time being, leaving aside the hurdles that he, like every innovator or visionary must overcome in pursuit of their revelatory ideas, Doctor Diego González would like to remind us here of the prison sentence and forced labor that Galileo suffered for saying that the Earth was round, not to mention the death of the discoverer of asepsis, Doctor Semmelweis, who was expelled from the international scientific community. He perished due to an infection caused by a cut on his skin when he was practicing an autopsy: paradoxes of science, or perhaps nothing more and nothing less than fate.

***

Leaving the obstacles behind, his evolution continued its course. After returning from Duke Medical Center, "while I practiced the dual port technique (or double incision) that I had learned, I realized that I was doing a Uniportal approach because most of the time I was working with the camera placed in the same orifice where I had inserted the instruments, because that's how I got a better view (first case in April 2009). So I thought, why not try to always insert the camera and surgical tools through the same incision, as if we were reproducing an open thoracotomy instrumentation? In June 2010, after thinking about it over and over again, I decided to do the first resection in the lower lobe through a single port. By inserting the tools and camera through one single opening, I realized that surgery was much more comfortable, I had much more visibility. This allowed us to be a lot faster. The post-operative progress of the patient was excellent. We released him the next day without any pain.

"This motivated me to further improve what I had just discovered. The first time I published it in an international medical journal, I did so by warning that the technique was only apt for lower lobes, and that I thought for the upper lobes, it would be necessary to have a new technology due to the angle of approach, that is, there was a physical obstacle to a clear view. However, soon as the technique progressed, I saw that if we positioned the lung differently than normal, we were also able to access the upper lobes, without needing new technology. We published all of our cases and results in the most prestigious thoracic surgery journals in 2011, and along with my team, we started to teach the technique to our closest colleagues, and to the residents that started it. In 2012, at an international conference, an Italian surgeon named Luca Bertolaccini, fascinated with our technique, concluded that the Uniportal VATS surgery was better than any other technique used by any of the best surgeons in the world. He summarized the difference by explaining that when inserting the tool and camera through the same single incision, we were able to achieve the same angle of view as in an open surgery. This mathematic explanation made me understand many things. For example, the reason for me feeling much more comfortable operating like that gave me the necessary assurance to teach Uniportal and reproduce its success around the world."

***

The tour begins: his exclusive, committed, generous and unpaid dedication to teaching Uniportal, which little by little would become a philosophy adopted by the most prestigious surgeons, who go to his bi-monthly trainings at Shanghai Pulmonary Hospital, or wherever Diego decides to go. He responds to all calls from the international medical community, by organizing conferences and giving master classes.

The first countries to invite him to give practical conferences and operate directly were China, Taiwan, South Korea, Russia, Israel, Indonesia, Brazil, Chile, Colombia, Turkey, United States, France, Italy and Germany. That was just the beginning. At the time, it seemed as though the surgeon had a special ability. It became a replicable technique that was exportable to the entire world. The international demand for courses grew with each day, and continues to grow, just like the never-ending travels that fill up his calendar.

CHAPTER 5:
The Three Cornerstones

Few dare to travel the world by themselves, to operate on extremely complex cases without a team.
I live to overcome.

"This is a story of how an idea gestates, and how it matures and becomes an innovation, and later a technique: a surgical technique that makes life better for people around the world," the doctor stated in his 2013 Ted Talk.

"It's a story based on three main cornerstones: firstly, a restless kid who from a very young age was curious about technology." This point is illustrated in his talk with a slide showing Diego as a 3-year-old boy, already near-sighted, peering at the camera through dark rimless glasses, sitting upright in a chair, holding the earpiece of a 70's-style bakelite telephone that was all the rage at that time, and in the other hand, a racing motorbike. "Secondly, an early interest in the sciences, particularly medicine; and thirdly, my affinity for water sports, especially surf, which made me aware that challenging oneself is important, that dreams can be reached, and that one can travel the world in search of waves, increasingly larger waves, and find in it a life philosophy. "But my urge to catch even bigger, and even more distant waves nearly cost me my life in 2005. It was the near-death experience that changed me and made me realize how important it is to know to measure risks and know your own limits."

Risk and destiny are two factors, one real and quantifiable, the other inexplicable and unimaginable, that are the roots of his biography, which grows like a vine around two stakes in the ground. The first time he met fate was in Bali, where he used to visit with his doctor's kit and a portable gurney on his back.

For ten years, he was also a volunteer doctor for the Spanish Surf Team, with whom he traveled the world. Diego's surf buddies remember and describe him as always taking risks, walking down the beach with a stretcher on his back and his first aid kit, always available to provide stitches, bandage, resuscitation, and anything needed. They dubbed him, "The Great Dieguini," and thus his surf nickname was born.

People on the beach and in specialized magazines glow with compliments about him. He's more than a local acquaintance; he's the leader, when it comes to dominating the waves, and the leader when the call comes through social media "There are good barrels at La Cueva" (barrel: ideal waves or surfing conditions in general). When this happens, 20 to 30 well-known surfers from A Coruña show up. Soon the sea erupts in a festival of waves that they ride, jump and carve. He is envied for his journeys to the most desired spots on the planet, for accompanying the National Team to championships, and for his anecdotes, stitching up the great ones, not to mention the locals, who used to go to his small, improvised surgery room he set up every season on the beaches of Bali: stitches and first aid.

We'll return to the Galician coasts, and also to the championships and his anecdotes, but let's stay in Bali, in the fateful month of October 2002. Diego is eating supper with a couple of friends in a restaurant in the touristy area of Kuta right in front of its idyllic beaches with crystal white sand. After dinner, they plan to go for a drink at the Sari Club, the most popular club in the area, in order to bid farewell to other friends who were returning home the next day. Some last-minute shopping delays them and they arrive late to their date with death. They are just 100 meters away when two deadly bombs explode at the door of the club, killing Diego's colleagues, who had arrived on time. A car bomb and another in a backpack littered the island's center of nightlife with death that October 12, taking the life of 202 people, and injuring another 209. "Seeing death so close, and being free of it by pure chance, just a few meters and barely three minutes, makes you rethink your fundamental values. Why did our friends die and not us?" At that time, Diego was a resident at Juan Canalejo, an R-3, still a baby. He was deeply affected; he started to take more risks, but 'calculated risks' as he prefers to say. Not many people dare to travel the world by themselves, to operate on extremely complex cases without a team. For me, I live to overcome."

He met fate again, shadowed by death, in Mentawai, Indonesia in 2005. Diego considers the incident to be a clear sign of his personality. "I went with some friends, including some professional surfers, to this Indonesian spot to look for the best waves in the world. They are enormous, super perfect waves that form in the middle of the sea. We spent two weeks on a boat, surfing all day, baked by the sun. It was the last day there and I remember I felt tired. But I saw one of those perfect waves coming, and the pro who caught it had fallen, leaving it open for me. I turned around and started riding it. It was enormous, with a huge tube, but when I tried to turn, I slipped. The wave engulfed me, and I started to roll over and over without being able to breathe until I completely ran out of air. I saw the tunnel, the light that precedes cerebral death. At the beginning, a lack of oxygen produces a feeling of pain, but then you reach a point where you relax, perhaps because it increases your carbon dioxide, and in that moment, I came up to the surface, landing on a coral reef. The wave had reached the sand and dissipated. I was really light-headed, but when I took a breath, I snapped back to life. There I realized the importance of knowing your own limits, measuring the risks and not exceeding your capacity. I had become too bold, catching bigger and bigger waves, but that wasn't the one for me: It was at least 13 feet tall. I've always been brave when surfing, and I tend to throw myself at waves that maybe aren't at my level, but after that incident, I now measure them much more. That experience taught me a lot, and has served in my life too, not just in sports."

It has helped him go beyond without being paralyzed by fear, measuring the risk. He has always thought of death as something natural that has to happen, "I'm very strong in face of it, tough, even when my elders, grandparents and aunts and uncles have died. I'm not afraid of my own death either, I've never been fearful, just somewhat unaware of the danger."

Extreme experiences have not occurred to him in vain. That's why Diego is an admirer of Ric Elias, an American who on January 15, 2009 sat in seat 1D on US Airways flight 1549 from La Guardia Airport in New York to North

Carolina. The plane had reached a height of 3,000 feet, and suddenly an explosion was heard. "Imagine a plane full of smoke and an engine making a terrifying noise, clack-clack-clack-clack". These are the first sentences of Elias' Ted Talk. In an harrowing eighteen-minute speech, he describes the scene like a horror film, with a final rush to rescue. The pilot veers the airplane, aligns it with the Hudson River, and cuts the engines. Two eternal minutes of silence and three cold words, "the most emotionless words I've ever heard in my life, 'Prepare for impact'". The landing on the Manhattan river which without a doubt will go into the history of aviation, saved the lives of all passengers and crew members. In his Ted Talk, Delta passenger 1D, who was born in Puerto Rico and is the CEO of a marketing agency, tells of three unique and important things that he thought of when he assumed he'd die in a matter of instants.

The first thing that passed through his mind was everything that he could have done and had left to do. "Everything can change in an instant. Each minute, you have to enjoy it because it could be your last," he said. Thus, he learned that you shouldn't put off what you want to do, just do it.

The second realization was the amount of time he had lost due to his ego. Since that moment, he has not again fought with his wife. "Between being right and being happy, I choose to be happy."

Thirdly, "Dying is not scary, it's as if we've always been preparing for it. But it is very sad because you love life. I was thinking that I wanted to see my children grow up."

Thanks to the pilot's expertise, a mere human being sitting only a couple of steps from the first-row seats, close enough to touch, he could watch his children grow for another six years. Now he travels the world, giving conferences, trying to transmit the real value of life.

Ric Elias summarizes what he learned in a question to the audience, a postscript for whoever wanted to hear it, "No one lives forever, but it's worth asking yourself, 'are you being the best person you can be?'"

***

It is not often that the questions and reflections of one person correspond to those of another, no matter how close. But in our essence, we are all just that: human beings with an inexorably finite amount of time.

Joaquín will never be able to forget what happened on the morning of February 2013 in the Pulmonology Department of Bellvitge Hospital of Barcelona. The doctor entered, carrying the results of his biopsy. "You can go home now, there's nothing left to do here." She was referring to the recurrence of cancer, now in his left lung.

"I felt an inexplicable emptiness. What I felt is inexplicable with words." A bottomless chasm had opened and was about to swallow him whole. "It's inexplicable what you feel in that moment," he repeats; "you feel impotent, a storm of anguish drags out all of your energy." Joaquín Silva Silva (then 54 years old) had had a tumor on his right lung operated on urgently around six years ago. A thoracotomy that curtailed the upper lobe of the organ and left him writhing in an indescribable pain for weeks, and then months.

The cancer came back four years later in a small node on the left lung. They treated it with chemotherapy, but the latest PET and biopsy results were devastating: the malignant cells had become immune, the node had grown, and the oncological team had run out of options.

How could he return home with that death sentence, and just accept it, as he faced his children, his grandchildren and other family? Later, Joaquín, his wife, Carmen Vargas, and their daughters drove to Empuriabrava, on the high coast of Girona; another car followed them with one of their nieces and her husband, who is like a son-in-law to him. Joaquín Silva is the patriarch of an extensive clan of Romani, they never travel alone. However, on that day, in addition to the family, "God was with us," said Carmen, who was sitting, impenetrable, in the back of the car, praying the same mantra she always heard from her father, "As long as there's hope, there's life." But hope, where to find it? Joaquín couldn't take the steering wheel, of course, but from the passenger's seat he said, "There must have been a mistake, this cannot be happening to me."

Everyone had heard talk about the latest surgical techniques for lung cancer aimed at a minimally invasive surgery. The technique would have benefitted Joaquín years ago after he had suffered an open-chest operation in which his thorax was sawed open from top to bottom, with the ribs folded in. As they followed behind him, the members of his family started searching online with their iPad, something that medical colleagues tend to discourage, if not prohibit. And that's what led them to him, Doctor Diego González. So simple, so unusual. Yet even more unusual was when Carmen and her daughters called the UCTMI (the Spanish acronym for Minimally Invasive Thoracic Surgery Unit) in A Coruña, it was Diego González himself who answered the phone. They told him their story and he didn't hesitate: "Send me the reports," he told them. Within an hour, they emailed them to him, and again, his voice on the phone said, "I want to see the patient." Carmen's face still lights up when she remembers that moment; her ragged eyes, with deep, dark circles, beam when she talks about Diego, Doctor Diego. Light emanating from a tired soul.

They didn't want to give the patriarch false hope, but the youngest daughter interjected: we have to tell him. They told him and the next day, they made their way to A Coruña.

They were like pilgrims on the way to Lourdes, holding on to the only possible, albeit remote, alternative: while there is hope, there is life. Three family members accompanied Joaquín to A Coruña for his appointment: his wife, his sister and her husband. Diego, Ricardo and a young German intern receive them. Neither the Bellvitge oncologists, nor the doctors who had operated on his first tumor, nor even the prestigious Baselga Institute, which they had also consulted, considered that his case was operable. The tumor's location on the hilum, his suffering of EPOC, the lobectomy that had already been performed (he only has 11% of his right lung) and the impact of the chemotherapy, made it an impossible case. Nobody gave him even the most minimal hope. Yet here was this young doctor telling them that yes, he'd operate on him. Carmen's face must have reflected her distrust and disbelief, which made the young German intern say, "But why such a face when he's telling you he's going to operate on your husband. He can save him!"

"How was I supposed to believe they could operate on him when all of the eminent people we had consulted had repeatedly told us that nothing could be done?" his wife explains now. "With all respect, I told them, 'it's just that this sounds like a story (the story I wanted to hear); and I can't believe it.' However, Diego has something special and he conveyed a confidence, such that..." Then it was Joaquín who asked the million-dollar question to Diego, "And how much is this going to cost? Because, of course, this is a private hospital. He responded, 'Don't worry about the money, it will be paid in some way, at some point.'" All of that was so different from what they had heard over the past six years of hell, it was so incredible. According to Joaquín, "Next, I dared to ask him the worst part, 'doctor, what do you think is the percentage that the operation will go well?'" To which Diego answers without hesitation, "It's not a question of percentages; rather, it's about possibilities, and you have many possibilities for it to go well."

***

We are in one of the restaurants owned by Joaquín, uncle Joaquín, Silva Silva, born into a family from Extremadura, who emigrated to Portugal fleeing the Spanish Civil War in 1936. The clan returned to their homeland (a clan that he prefers to call an extended family) in 1970. They established themselves in the prosperous area of Girona; they had acquired the tough and hard-working spirit of the Portuguese. Joaquín, the younger of the 11 Silva Silva brothers, started as a waiter at age 17, and ended up being a cook and restaurant owner. At El Capitán, the headquarters of his hospitality business, where we are now, between the beach and the port, he has a precious photo of himself with celebrated chef Ferran Adrià and other local cooks from the Gulf of Roses, leaning on boats and fishing nets. He has another one with equally famous chefs Subijana and Arzak. The family now controls the restaurant which looks like it should be on a postcard, with a fishing net draped over a boat, and tools to hunt octopus. He says it's a business of passion more than money. He also has a second business, specializing in cured Spanish *jamón* (ham), which proudly features a huge photo of his oldest granddaughter over the door, "She's just beautiful." The patriarch has this second and a third business as well.

It's post-meal coffee time at El Capitán, and the restaurant is gradually emptying. Two stunningly beautiful daughters and the aforementioned oldest granddaughter make their appearance. The girl behaves politely amidst the torpor of this dense adult conversation, despite not wanting to hear anything (in reality, she only wants to hear that she deserves an ice cream for behaving so well). "We returned home, I did the pre-operation tests, and to add insult to injury, one week later, during Easter of 2013, I was in the operating room." A caravan, including his two daughters and their respective husbands, the nephew who rules El Capitán, some of Joaquín's 11 brothers, the youngest and most spoiled, the great entrepreneur, the respected boss, all accompanied him to the occasion of the surgery. "There were 15 of us in total; Joaquín and I traveled one day beforehand in order to get admitted to the hospital," his wife says. He went in the operating room, and everyone was in the waiting room. How many hours? They don't know. Some hours pass like eternities. Perhaps it was three or four hours in total. "What I do know for sure is that they had told me the longer the time, the better, because if they called us right away, it was because they couldn't do anything. Time was passing in our favor," said one of his daughters with an overwhelming brightness.

Who delivered the news to you in the operating room, and what did they say? It's an emotional question, because its answer is the key to an entire possible future. "You're clean! They've cleaned you up! It went well!" said the daughters in the hallway that goes from the operating room to the recovery room: Joaquín, still waking up from the anesthesia, in that limbo space that conflates dream and reality, Carmen crying, the son-in-law crying, all in tears, wailing. They had been waiting for that moment in the room, and now the daughters rejoiced with their mother. The men were in the waiting room, at the door to the operating room, where signs prohibited them from going any farther: entry forbidden for all non-medical personnel. Diego ended up confessing that that experience impacted him. "Imagine it! Imagine the scene if the operation had gone wrong." It was an operation plagued with danger and suspense; at one point, only the 11% left of his right lung was functioning.

When Carmen went down to the room, she found Diego leaving the operating room, saying goodbye. "It went well. There was one complicated moment, still we were able to clean everything up."

"We were all waiting for the 'but,'" said the youngest daughter, Remedios; and it was just like, 'but...' Everyone was waiting to hear them say 'but,' but there was no 'but.'" He explained the operation in detail, and they nicknamed him 'The Rescue Surgeon.' Joaquin's sister stretched her body around Diego and began to jump while hugging him.

Carmen spent that night next to her husband in the recovery room. After a few hours, he was fully aware of what she was saying: he was clean. The family went out to celebrate, to paint the town red, and he and his wife could finally relax. "The next day was Good Friday. Who would have imagined that a doctor would come see a patient on one of the biggest holidays of the year? He came, sat at the foot of Joaquín's bed, and started talking with us with a simplicity and humility that I'll never forget: this gesture will forever be ingrained in my heart."

Two days after the operation, Carmen and Joaquín walked along the beach of Riazor, avoiding the subject that for months —six months— had them living on pins and needles. When the result of the first CAT scan arrived, they finally dared to speak about healing: that's when they started to talk about the future again. Until today, three years later, counting the days until completing the five symbolic years until they pronounced you healed. "Our gratitude to Diego is something that cannot be expressed with words: he has given our lives back," they all say, more or less in unison, as they head for home, along those streets that are like piers over the water, in that small town waterlogged by sea, Empuriabrava.

CHAPTER 6:
What Really Matters

I'm not God: I cannot lose my objectivity and disregard the
oncological principle that governs surgeries.

When the patient wakes up in the recovery room, they anxiously look for a face and an answer. Sometimes, that face would be Diego's, in whom the patient had put his entire hope for life. However, normally it's not Diego who is there, instead, it's the anesthesiologist. They have to check that the patient is 'making a good recovery'. That is, the patient is alert, with it and conscious, wishing with their whole soul that you'll give them the best news. The kind face of César Bonome, the team's anesthesiologist, is usually the one to appear and tell him, "I'm the man of your dreams, the surgery was successful."

And if it wasn't, then what do you tell them? "That the surgeons will let them know, because they're the ones who know. The doctors even have the patients' cell phone numbers and end up being friends with them. And I'm talking about the entire team (Diego, Ricardo, Mercedes), this team's manner is so intimate, so unusual...There's always an additional stress when the patient has come looking for their last chance at life, because operating on a cancer is not an aesthetic touch-up, or anything comparable, rather it's life or death," Bonome continued. "Diego makes the decision to operate. The family is outside the surgery room, waiting for him to tell them, 'Everything went well.' The first thing a patient looks for when they wake up is his face, to ask him how the operation went." In other words, the patient wants to know if they are going to be saved.

"But I've also seen Diego's face when midway through an operation, he discovers that the tumor is more complicated than he thought, because it's not removable or has infiltrated veins or has metastasized beyond the diagnosis in the tests. You can tell in his gestures, that feeling of defeat; after having spent three hours trying, he feels a personal failure, even though that's far from the truth." It's the small cemetery of surgeons, which the British neurosurgeon Henry Marsh humbly recounts in his beautiful memoirs, *Do No Harm*. "But luckily this only happens in approximately 10% of his cases, which is compensated for by the 90% of successful surgeries."

***

We spend the morning talking over breakfast and coffee in the San Rafael Hospital cafeteria, where the UCTMI has its operating base. The center is adjacent to the CHUAC, where the consultant surgeon Doctor González Rivas is working three days of shifts and surgeries. We're going to meet him. Between appointments and operating rooms, Diego is glued to his cell phone, on which he receives a message. A patient has written him, showing him his case, adding a postscript after the message.

"Please help me. I have two young sons and an 18-month-old daughter."

"It breaks my heart," he says as he reads the message out loud, and responds, "You must know that those facts cannot influence my decision, because then I would be doing something inappropriate, but I promise I'll do everything to help you."

"You can't lose your objectivity," he explains. "It's very difficult to face situations like that. It is especially essential to not lose sight of the oncological principle that governs most of our surgeries. There is a series of protocols established by consensus, which is necessary to follow, and these indicate when surgery is advisable and when it isn't, as it wouldn't be of any benefit because of the phase or state the tumor is in.

"Normally, the cases we handle have come looking for a second opinion, or are tumors that in other centers, they didn't dare operate on because they considered them to be very technically complex. Occasionally, patients have been offered open surgery, but the patient is looking for minimally invasive, closed surgery. Alternatively, in the reference center the case has been rejected, because they're not familiar with video-assisted surgery and the patient is not a candidate for an open surgery, which is infinitely more aggressive.

"When the difficulty is with the technique because the tumor is located in a difficult-to-access or high-risk area, due to our great experience and involvement in developing video-assisted surgery we sometimes take it and operate because we feel that we can. We operate on tumors that show up after chemotherapy and radical radiotherapy, those that are in contact with the vena cava or other large veins and imply broncovascular reconstructions or the removal of the carina that had been rejected elsewhere due to the high degree of difficulty they entail. In these cases, we practice what could be called a VATS rescue surgery. However, on other occasions, patients come to us in desperation, believing that we can operate on everything: they've heard that at UCT-MI, we've operated on other terminally ill patients, and no matter what, they want to be operated on. Obviously, we are not gods, and we respect the oncological principles. If they have advanced metastasis or multiple ganglion stations are affected, for example, despite being able to remove their tumor, surgery wouldn't be the best option. In that case, as painful as it is to say it, we must be very clear and explain: the tumor is non operable. Those are obviously really tough moments, but the surgeon cannot be too influenced by any one factor, such as the young age of the patient, or the family members begging; we never can do that, because it would lead to incorrect recommendations. We cannot get started with that game, and regrettably, we have to reject some because they're not suitable for surgery; it's one thing to remove it, which we could do, but if it's not recommended due to the metastasis, the operation would not offer survival.

"We cannot cure cases that do not have a solution, nor can we say yes to everything, obviously; if nothing else, we must respect the surgical recommendation. We are very selective about the decision to operate in the cases that come to us looking for a second opinion."

***

"We're going to change the history of thoracic surgery —Uniportal VATS is the future!" The words of Doctor

Bonome sound legendary in the documentary *This is life*, directed by Daniel López, which tells of the first journeys of the surgeon González Rivas to teach his single port technique:

"A thoracotomy involved an 18-centimeter incision that Uniportal VATS reduces to two or three centimeters, and also does not expose the cavities and organs, because it is a closed operation, you keep them in place. Open surgery requires very complex anesthesia techniques that protect the patient. You need the patient to be profoundly asleep, with a tube in the trachea, a collapsed lung and mechanical ventilation. However, it has been shown that:

"1) When a patient is anesthetized so deeply, there is greater risk of post-operation death and cognitive dysfunction. There are even patients who after an intervention like that never return to be the same. Why? Because there are anesthetic agents that when administered at such a high concentration, produce a certain degree of neural death. That's why it's so important to minimize the dose of the anesthetic drugs.

"2) The open surgical techniques are very aggressive and painful and cause a general reaction in the body: it is not harmless to open an abdomen or thorax. It produces endocrine, catabolic, stress and inflammatory responses. The patient takes months to return to their normal state.

"3) The neuromuscular paralysis that is required for the surgery causes worse pulmonary function during recovery.

"4) Mechanical ventilation implies lung damage, which even if it's microscopic, also has its price and consequences.

"Anesthesiologists with Uniportal VATS only need a peripheral regional blockage, minimal sedation and on occasion, we don't even put a tube in them, nor do we need mechanical ventilation. All of this combined translates into additional protection for the patient, who clearly feels it in their recovery and progress. We practically see no post-operation complications, when before the incidence of complications was fairly significant. Normally, the patient stayed one or two days in the ICU and then two weeks in the hospital. Now the patient can return to their private room after spending two hours in the recovery room, and 48 hours later, they are discharged from the hospital, because really, the only thing they need is to wake up, recover and gain control.

"The Uniportal surgical technique, which also allows this type of sedation and peripheral regional blockage is an obvious revolution for general surgery. In the case of thoracic surgery, it goes much quicker, but that is exclusively due to the characteristics of the pioneer, Diego. The future, without a doubt, is for the minimal invasion possible — that is, Uniportal."

Why does Uniportal stand out so much when there was already a two- and three-port approach? "Because in thoracic video-assisted surgery, each incision must be locally covered with analgesic. It is much more complicated and harmful to anesthetize three ports rather than just one. As for the cost, I think public health departments should seriously study it. The thoracotomy requires one to two days in the ICU, which cost the institution 2,000 to 4,000 euros, plus one to two weeks in a private room. There is intense pain and greater risk of infection and post-surgery complications, with all the danger that this entails, plus the costs of drugs and staff. So Uniportal VATS not only improves the recovery and well-being of the patients, but it's obviously very economically viable."

***

César Bonome is nearly 10 years older than Diego and the average of the three surgeons on the team, but it was clear to him from the first time he saw Diego perform a surgery. "It was as if he were my godchild. From his first steps as a resident, I believed in him. After a brief learning curve, Diego perfected the technique, and since then, he has dedicated his life to teach and disseminate it. If it weren't that way, and he didn't do it with such enthusiasm, infusing so many surgeons around the world with the desire to learn, the surgical progress would be much slower. If he were sitting in his office, the process wouldn't be reaching the whole world, and that's his great achievement."

He went on, "His achievement was to perfect the technique, his philanthropic labor of teaching it around the world. Very few people would be willing to dedicate their lives to it." Like a monk, it's a crusade.

"The recognition of the international scientific community is his only compensation, because of course, he doesn't benefit financially from it: for him, it would be much more profitable to get established in a private hospital in any place in the world, which would bring him patients and he would charge to operate on them. However, today, 95% of his operations are totally free. That is, when he goes to operate in a country like, let's say, South Africa, Chile or China, he doesn't charge anything; unless the visit is organized by the surgical instrument industry, which pays for his travel and sometimes very small stipends, for service.

His teaching is purely philanthropic, for adventure and personal learning: he never knows what he'll find wherever he goes.

"I admire Diego's bravery. When he applied his technique for the first time here, after operating on barely three cases, he went to Mount Sinai of New York to present how he had done it in a forum of super demanding American surgeons. He was barely 36 years old, and that was a huge challenge, in the face of a community as rigid as the American thoracic surgeons. But he was totally sure of what he was doing."

***

The rest of the team don't hesitate to praise him for being a pioneer and crusader: Mercedes de la Torre (current head of the unit) and Ricardo Fernández (the baby brother, one year younger than Diego: they look like brothers because of their young physical appearance) saw it clearly from the beginning. "His dedication to teaching is admirable. He travels blindly many times, not knowing what cases he'll find, what material and medical equipment he'll have, what the hospital conditions will be."

Ricardo recounts the before and after of Uniportal VATS in the oncological process. "When we used to operate on advanced cases which had previously been given chemotherapy, it was normal that the patient wouldn't survive an open thoracotomy. Now they recover from Uniportal without complications. Or the reverse situation, where most patients you operate on with open surgery, later couldn't complete the subsequent chemical treatments, due to the condition they were in: the less surgical aggression, the smaller the change of the immunological resistance. This surgery is so minimally aggressive that it allows you to complete the treatments if necessary." Curative, rescue surgery.

CHAPTER 7:
That Untamable Child

I was horrified to see the patients writhing in pain. It seemed so aggressive: opening up a chasm in them, separating their ribs...I felt like I was going backwards to advance science. Life is full of wrong predictions. In 1913, the American bank advised Henry Ford to not invest in the automobile, because the horse would always be the principle means of transportation.

By the time he reached middle school, he stood out as a leader. His rebellion knew no bounds. Nothing stood in the way of little Diego's drive and boldness: not even the dark rimmed glasses he wore as a child to correct a slight squint (and which he later needed again because of his myopia) made him seem inferior in the eyes of his peers. He never had a single complex either, not even during puberty.

"I was the boldest, most daring kid," the now mature man reflects. "I was an *argalleiro*," which in Galician means something like a trickster, inventor of stories and games, a teaser. This curious Galician term takes us to his childhood roots, in the gypsy neighborhood of Penamoa, on the outskirts of A Coruña. News is spreading that the Royal Academy of the Spanish Language has removed the discriminatory and offensive use of "gypsy" and "gypped": trickster and tricked.

However, Diego was the king of the *argalleiros*, he confesses slyly, proud yet graceful. He was the head of a gang of gypsies, the Penamoa gang. "My grandparents lived in a house outside the city (that has since been dismantled and their inhabitants relocated). When I was little, starting around the age of 10, I stayed with my grandparents most weekends, and '*argallando*' around the area, I discovered the gypsy population, and I started spending time with them. I became friends with the kids, and they took me to have snacks in their houses, which were shacks. I got to know their families, and in the end, I became the top dog. Looking back, I don't understand how my parents agreed to it, but I do remember the kids yelling up to my grandma's house: 'Heyyyyy, Juliaaaa' (said in a perfect gypsy *caló* accent), 'tell Diego to come down!' Because I always thought of entertaining things to do, and they loved hanging out with me. There was an abandoned quarry, and I remember I told them, 'I want to go to the top,' and they said, 'you're crazy, don't do it!' I risked my life and reached the very top —nobody followed me. I was a hero. I remember one time there were these bushes loaded with ripe blackberries, which were in a place that was extremely difficult to reach, between rocks and gorse: 'No, Diego! You're crazy!' they told me. And that time I didn't make it. I fell in a deep and dark cave, I don't even know how deep. The neighbors had to come and rescue me with ropes, but before they could get there, I still remember feeling the snakes slithering under my feet, snakes and all types of bugs. I was trapped there between gorse and bushes that were clinging to me: Imagine what it was like until they got me out of there. Later, I couldn't sleep alone, because I'd wake up in the middle of the night, and I'd see bugs everywhere, biting me."

At that time, Penamoa was a supermarket of drugs, in the hard years of Galician narco-trafficking, a bit like Cañada Real Galiana today in Madrid. This situation was one of the main causes of the demolition of the neighborhood and eventual relocation of its inhabitants, which took no less than a decade to achieve. "But my friends and their families were good. I thought they were really good guys —the kids who did drugs were in a different area. Now when I think about it, I wonder how they let me go out, but it's true that if they had forbidden it, I would have done it anyway, because I was tremendously rebellious. Sometimes, I wonder what happened to those people, those kids I used to lead when we were 10, 12 years-old. I remember back at the "*Bienve,*" there was a kid missing an eye, a really good guy. I think my parents and my grandparents let me hang out with them because they were really good people, they couldn't see that there was any danger." The danger was more him, it seems. He shells his stories like peas from a pod —like the time he traded his glasses for candies and proudly showed off: "Mom, look what I got!" Little Diego, who was not only near-sighted, but also suffered a slight squint, which they corrected, although the traces on his deep and scrutinizing face still remains.

***

His grades at a private, elite school called Obradoiro were just high enough. "I was good at math, physics and other sciences, but I wasn't interested in studying at all, it seemed like a pain to have to memorize for classes. I liked jokes. I'd record them on cassette tapes, holed up for hours in my room, just 6 years-old. I still have a few of them, and when you hear them, you'll die of laughter. I wanted to be a movie star." He unleashed all of his childhood imagination on monologues that he'd later present before the audience of his family and relatives: the child was an orchestra of words.

His childhood of jokes came and went, as did Penamoa. In his teen years, he developed a passion for the sea, always looking for new adventures. Surfing was and is his means of escape, his way of releasing tension and relaxing. It also provides exercise at the same time and he enjoys the continuous challenge. In addition to his passion for surgery, Doctor González likened his love for surf to "that girlfriend who keeps stringing you along, until you're hooked. With waves, like surgery, you never know what you're going to find, what is going to happen."

He never forgot his taste for risk and speed, motorcycles nor his flirtation with bungee-jumping —an episode that Diego remembers well. "I have a great friend named Alfonso, who is a climber and now works for the United Nations in London. One day, he arrived from France with a new idea. We were 16 years-old." The new idea was that extreme sport that consists of jumping into a void, hundreds of meters down, from a bridge, or something similar, with the torso or feet attached to an elastic rope; something which was still unknown in Spain. "And we went to Lugo to try it, without knowing anything. We set up the climbing ropes we had, even though bungee-jumping ropes are much more elastic. We tied them to the bridge deck with a blanket in between so that the rope wouldn't fray against the concrete, and we jumped. The first to do it was Alfonso, who jumped off feet first, and the next day, I did it head first, without even knowing how the rope was going to respond (he has saved a video of one of those jumps on his cell phone —it is shocking). The people who passed by looked at us with amazement, and one day the police came. We went several times." Diego doesn't like to say he's brave, but "do you understand me now?" is how he summarizes it. He has done base jumping, skydiving and all types of sports involving risk, speed and height, anything that gets his adrenaline pumping (and he continues to do them, when he can).

He carried on like this until his calling came, knock-ing on his door with enough force to re-awaken the child-hood dreams he had long forgotten. His mother, however, does remember, because her memory goes back farther. His mother was a postpartum nurse, formerly a midwife, and was very popular and beloved in the A Coruña Maternal and Children's Hospital, an employee of the same CHU-AC where he currently works. "I used to really like going to see her at the hospital. I also had a family doctor who without a doubt inspired that passion inside me: I loved to talk with him and visit him at the office. I always liked medicine, the power to heal fascinated me, but I was so restless and rebellious that really, I wasn't conscious of it."

That was the case until it came time to choose my cours-es, and there he realized his hidden fascination. "I loved when my mother told me things about the hospital. I'd spend the whole day asking her questions. Also, as a kid, I had a lot of throat problems. I always had to go to the ENT. I hated going to the doctor as a patient, I even re-fused to let them give me stitches one day to sew up a cut on my finger; there was no way they were going to suture me. But I entertained myself by going through the Medi-cation Guides of everything they prescribed for my throat

81

and ears, and I was able to pick a few things up." These are vague memories Diego pieces together as he speaks, but no, he was not the model child destined for one vocation, and one vocation only. That's impossible, taking into account his restless and versatile personality.

We are sitting and talking in the big house he lives alone in, on a rainy afternoon. He remembers how from an early age he played roller hockey, the most popular sport amongst A Coruña's youth, on the city's star team: Liceo Caixa Galicia, always among the top of the league. He moves in this world alone, but is never lonely: wherever he goes, he is praised by the masses. His last serious relationship ended when that chapter we titled "Obstacles" came to a head, in reaction to which, he started a global crusade to disseminate Uniportal VATS (the 2013-2014 academic year). The relationship had become unstable, and although their memories and friendship continue to be wonderful, "My head is in another place right now. I can't think about a relationship; everything has it's time and place. For the last three years, I've gotten used to being alone, and I am enjoying it. I'm happy this way. My life today doesn't allow me to have a stable relationship, I'm always looking for a change." It will come. Diego (42 years-old) would love to have a family and children, and he hopes to have them, "I just haven't found the woman for that, and I'm not looking for her right now."

We were talking about Diego's last year of school when he was seriously considering the future and what he was going to be. His interest was undoubtedly in the sciences. It was the only subject he put effort into learning. Thus, in the guidance talks for university, he decided on medicine, although he admits that then he didn't have a particular calling to care or heal others. "No, I still wasn't thinking about that; I discovered that later when I started specializing in thoracic surgery."

The time also came to stop being so scattered and to focus on getting good grades in order to get accepted to university —no trivial task at the time. "No, until then I hadn't been outstanding, and to study medicine, I had to be. You had to be the typical outstanding student, but I was always very atypical. It was only after listening to those talks and guidance tutorials that I decided that I wanted to be a doctor."

So he starts to focus because he is meant to be something in this life. A vocation that he wasn't even aware of, was born. No, medicine wasn't his vocation, it was something else. Perhaps it was fate.

**

He has long, thin hands that could play piano, but have instead preferred to handle lades, saws, staples, scalpels and needles, getting stained with blood and saving lives: a surgeon's hands and eagle eyes.

In the first lessons in Pathological Anatomy, the students were divided into groups by table. The tables were made of zinc and on top of them, there would be a cold cadaver like a block of ice. Diego was fascinated by one cavity in the human body —the cavity of the soul or the last breath, the thoracic box that encloses the heart and lung. He decided to pursue studying the latter, maybe because the first transplant of the heart had happened long ago, but the first one for the lungs was soon to come.

The British Neurosurgeon Henry Marsh wrote in his acclaimed book of memoirs *Do No Harm* that to be a surgeon, one must be capable of a certain amount of violence. "Having spent six months watching surgeons operating I decided that this was what I should do. I found its controlled and altruistic violence deeply appealing," confessed Marsh. Diego disagrees, he does not at all share the opinion of his wise and respected colleague. "No. It's not true that surgeons have to be violent. You do need to lose your inhibition, but you do not need aggression, and certainly not violence. You need to lose your inhibition to cause damage in pursuit of a benefit: you assume the risk. However, you can be the biggest pacifist in the world and accept that you have to cause that damage because you know your only purpose is beneficial." He gives as an example his colleague in the department, Mercedes de la Torre Bravos, one of his most faithful followers and a co-participant since the beginning in Uniportal VATS, (like the anesthesiologist, César Bonome, also known as the man of your dreams, and Ricardo Fernández Prado). "Mercedes didn't like doing it either (he's using the past tense, referring to the open thoracotomy); she's delicate, demure, very calm, but she would reach the operating room and have to do it."

The thoracotomy was his worst nightmare. "I hated it. I hate it even now when I have to perform a transplant, because open surgery is still the only way to carry out a transplant. It's a super aggressive surgery. The open thoracotomy made me feel like I was going backwards in advancing science."

He insists on refuting "that controlled violence" which Marsh referred to as the basis of his attraction to surgery, because refusing to accept violent surgery was precisely the leitmotif guiding him to becoming a visionary surgeon. Eliminating the pain of thoracotomy patients was his great rebellion, his positive revolt. "I was horrified when I saw the patients writhing in pain. It's such an aggressive surgery in and of itself, that I couldn't take it anymore: opening up a chasm, separating the ribs... One must be capable of such surgical aggression, but it made me feel very bad. I couldn't accept it. Neither could I accept that the surgery would continue to be so painful in the post-operating room and could even produce chronic thoracic pain, as a result of separating the ribs mechanically, because the nerves are sometimes affected. The thoracotomy is the most painful incision of all surgeries, and it is, let's say, the negative part of my specialization."

He rebelled, researched, and when he finally found video-assisted surgery being done elsewhere, he didn't want to waste another minute. "I have to learn this now," he said in 2007. He had been a consultant surgeon in the department for barely two years.

It is because of his determination to fight against pain that Uniportal VATS has transformed into a philosophy, a school, a mantra.

It's printed on their shirts. After each one of his courses, the most illustrious thoracic surgeons in the world put on a t-shirt that reads, "Keep calm and think Uniportal!"

***

Diego does not remember facing any obstacles in his life as a student, nor growing up, nor later in the Faculty of Medicine of Santiago de Compostela. "In medical school, we had great camaraderie. They respected me because I wasn't a nerd, I studied two days before the exam, but I got the highest grades. I didn't have to work very hard. The rest of the time, I spent traveling, surfing; it gave the others a bit of healthy jealousy, and they'd tease me. I worked as a bartender. People remember me at the bar with my notes, studying on the nights before my exams, even on the day before the medical specialization entrance examination. For me, the bar was freedom, because I found it unbearable to be locked up for the entire day. It helped, of course, that I never liked alcohol. I've always been a very healthy and athletic person, although now I've learned to appreciate a good wine.

"Earning money pouring drinks at night is something that started when I was just a teen. Because my mother was a nurse, and had a lot of night shifts, my sister and I grew up in my aunt's house, but during the day, we were with my parents. My aunt lived in the center of A Coruña, and already at the age of 15 or 16 years old, I escaped at night to come and work here (we are in front of the mythical club in A Coruña, Playa Club, on the sand in front of the sea of Riazor). Perhaps that's where my gift with people was born, and my desire to know (which for Diego started long ago). I was always surrounded by people older than me. I'd ask them about their experiences in life; I loved being behind the bar, and I learned a ton of things. Yes, I was always precocious.

"Working in pubs and clubs, I was able to earn money to travel and surf; which was one of my earliest passions. Looking for waves and finding the best have also driven me since I decided to study medicine. I wanted to be surrounded by the best, in everything. I got better with the best, and I learned from them, which is something I continue to apply to my life."

He also continued to work nights. Diego's trademark was having his notes open at the bar at LP45, packed with students from Compostela in the neighboring city of Órdenes. Not long ago, he received an email from a fellow student he barely remembered, saying, "Congratulations for your achievements. I still remember you studying at night in the bar at LP."

And of course, there were the girls. "Working at a club also allowed me to meet many girls (his love life has always been unstable), and I'd dress up nicely, with my longish hair... I never stopped surfing in the morning, to get energized and because it helped to balance my mind, and even prepare for my medical specialization exams. Thanks to surfing, I'd have the pure concentration to study five hours a day. I'm a very practical person." He passed his medical specialization entrance exams with a good enough grade to be comfortably accepted into the specialty of thoracic surgery, for which in that year, 1999, there were only seven spots available in all of Spain. "I was always fascinated by the thoracic cavity. Operating inside the chest was something that excited me." He was the first resident in the Juan Canalejo Hospital to be trained in lung transplants.

***

Think differently, because nothing is impossible. It has been his philosophy for as long as he can remember. Turning obstacles into incentives to transform negatives into positives ("a life free of obstacles is a life without success"). For Doctor González Rivas, the term 'impossible' doesn't exist: it's a synonym of nothing, absolute zero.

"I don't remember obstacles in either my childhood or my teen years, which were very happy and creative; not even in my university years did I face many obstacles. But I ended up defining my philosophy when I started to work at the hospital, when I discovered the miseries of the working world."

He also says it in an article published in the Journal of Thoracic Disease in August 2014. In the article, he talks about the years from when he started his crusade against unacceptable pain and damage that open surgery causes in lung patients, until when he was able to develop and apply the video-assisted surgical technique via a single portal or incision, Uniportal VATS (2007-2010) which gave such optimal results.

"During this entire time, we had to face many obstacles: it wasn't a bed of roses. When you design a new technique, you also need to develop new mechanisms to apply it. In this case, a new approach to the lung, new surgical protocol and how to teach it to the rest of the team. But it's not just that, you must also face the reluctance of prestigious surgeons who feel threatened by a new technique, and perhaps are no longer in conditions to learn and apply them. Envy and criticism arise. Any innovation involves restrictions and opposition, always. But these obstacles make us grow. We had to endure criticism from some colleagues who doomed us to failure, such as, 'you'll never get anywhere, this technique has no future,' but it has collapsed in face of the evidence.

"Life is full of erroneous predictions. In 1913, the President of the Bank of Michigan advised the founder of the Ford Company, Henry Ford, to not invest in what at that time was the incipient automotive industry. In his view, the horse would always be the means of transportation for humans, and the car was simply a fleeting trend. Luckily,

Ford didn't heed the banker's advice. He invested, became a multi-millionaire and the rest is history.

"My team has always followed the philosophy of not letting ourselves be intimidated by obstacles and to remain open to progress, because one never knows what the future may hold. The coming generation will operate with robots, through a single incision, and with wireless cameras. We are sure of that because the future of surgery is in minimally invasive approaches. For that reason, from the beginning we believed firmly in our idea. Who knows if in the not too distant future we will have robotic surgery devices which we will activate remotely, from our own house, for example. We cannot deny progress, and make negative predictions, holding onto 'that's how it's always been done.'"

"I've learned that in life, if you walk alone, you go faster, but if you let others accompany you, you go farther. Without the support of the people that love us and if we didn't have such a great team, we wouldn't have reached where we are. Who could have told us that from a small corner of this peninsula that is Spain, with so many colleagues committed to our innovation, after so much work, dedication and trust that we were going to revolutionize thoracic surgery around the world? That's why I think it's important to not stop thinking differently, and not to abandon an idea if you are convinced that it is important. I firmly believe that the key is: think differently, measure the risk, be innovative, believe in an idea, fight for it and overcome the obstacles, because *impossible is nothing*."

He then went on to cite Stephen Hawking, "Intelligence is the ability to adapt to changes."

***

The surgical team is like a small family, but not in a cliché sort of manner. It consists of the surgeons González Rivas, De la Torre and Fernández Prado; always attended by the anesthesiologist César Bonome of the Minimally Invasive Thoracic Surgery Unit (UCTMI[1]); accompanied in the department at Juan Canalejo Hospital by María Delgado and Eva Fieira; rotational staff, residents, aides and operating room nurses, as well as the invaluable secretary of the service, Pilar Núñez. They make up the team, or as they call it in Spain, the 'equipo,' which is fitting in the etymological sense of the word. It comes from the Old French word équiper, which in the Middle Ages first meant "to embark upon," and later came to mean "to provide the ship whatever necessary." Thus, equipo: "essential to create whatever is needed," says Diego. "Our service is very family-like, which is not very common in a public hospital, and especially one the size of CHUAC[2] (A Coruña University Hospital Complex, with Juan Canalejo as its emblem). It's also interesting, because at Shanghai Pulmonary, I'm finding the same thing —a team that is increasingly united around the Uniportal philosophy."

---

1. *Unidad de Cirugía Torácica Mínimamente Invasiva*, in Spanish.
2. *Complejo Hospitalario Universitario de A Coruña*, in Spanish.

CHAPTER 8:
Obstacles

The obstacles that life puts in your way happen for a reason.
Through them, you get to know yourself
and your limits, to reflect, and in my case, to conclude that
impossible is nothing.

In every story, the time for this chapter comes. Besides being a reality, obstacles are the Gordian knot and propeller of the story being told; because perhaps if this would not have happened, Diego would not have had to make the great obstacle of his career into a positive event: *keep calm and think Uniportal!*

"The obstacles life puts in your way happen for a reason. I'm convinced of this," he says, "and through them, you get to know yourself and your limits, to reflect, and in my case, to conclude that impossible is nothing." Nothing, a noun that indicates what does not exist.

He chose his specialization in 1999. At the time, he was vacillating between thoracic and cardiac surgery, and plastic surgery was also appealing. However, he decided on thoracic surgery because, among other things, at that time they had started to practice lung transplants in A Coruña. A resident surgeon in Valencia had just arrived at the Juan Canalejo Hospital, with the purpose of setting up a program in A Coruña —known as the Herculine city. Diego remembers clearly the exact day he chose to accept the residency there. He was in Madrid, it was 11:00 in the morning and in two hours, his flight was leaving for South Africa. He was going there to surf at Jeffrey's Bay, a tiny town on the Eastern Province of the Cape where the waves are famous worldwide: a site of pilgrimage for surfers. He went alone, because he wanted to be by himself and reflect. He stayed at a backpacker's hostel where there were only surfers. At that time, Diego's priority in life was to catch waves. "How things change," he thinks out loud. "Now, for me, life is about enjoying surgery and disseminating Uniportal around the planet."

When he was in Jeffrey's Bay, news was published about the first transplant in A Coruña. He remembers it because his mother had sent him a letter with the article cut out. The surgeon, who had arrived from Valencia and, and had been appointed Head of Department, had carried it out with his new team at the hospital, which at that time was called Juan Canalejo (today it is called CHAUC). When Diego returned, he was going to be his first resident with a position in thoracic surgery solely based on his medical specialization exams. In addition to that, and more importantly, it meant that he was the first surgeon trained in lung transplants in Galicia. He arrived full of excitement, yet still, from the very first instant he found out who would be his future teacher, his intuition told him they wouldn't get along. He wouldn't see a teacher in him, but something else. Cold shoulder: that's how the man acted toward his first resident (R1) in that position, his first student starting from the very beginning.

The team quickly identified the reason for the recently arrived boss's coldness and distant attitude: his life's goal was none other than to serve his own self, his own ego. He cared little about the assistants, rotation staff and residents of the service. There was something highly odd apparent to the team: when any of them went to a laboratory to request their operation be presented at a conference, a course or similar event (something that in Spain is generally financed by the pharmaceutical industry and the laboratories, because that is how they train doctors), the pharmaceutical representatives always replied that the training funds had already been disbursed to a foundation that was supposedly in charge of the scientific development of the service. Later, they were stunned to discover that the recipient of the funds was the Better without Tobacco Foundation. It was effectively a foundation —which although it did exist— created and directed by the same chief doctor for his own personal benefit from the resources that the pharmaceutical industry sent to develop the entire thoracic surgery service in the public hospital of A Coruña.

Despite the lack of encouragement from his boss, which meant very little rotation, learning or innovation was happening, Diego started to become interested in video-assisted surgery. At the end of 2006, he asked for permission for a one-month educational leave. He combined this with other weeks of vacation and was able to get a rotation at Cedar Sinai Hospital of Los Angeles to learn alongside the great Doctor McKenna, the father of video-assisted thoracic surgery. Thus, his journey toward allowing others to live without pain began.

Diego returned from Los Angeles with excitement, and immediately started to implement video-assisted surgery at

Juan Canalejo Hospital. His boss allowed him to purchase the necessary materials, and one day, he went with him to the operating room: Diego guided the operation, and the doctor attended as Head of Department. There was no way he was going to let a consulting surgeon perform an innovative operation within his department by himself, but he wasn't going to block it either. "At the beginning, he was open and willing, and he accepted it, which was positive. But then I started to claim my own patients and pursue my own independence in the operating room. I read and studied a lot, I watched lots of video-assisted surgery, and in 2008, I decided to do another rotation, this time at Memorial Hospital in New York. There I met a resident from Duke University Medical Center who did the drawing for me that became my obsession: they were operating through two single ports. From there, on my next vacation break, I went to Duke, where I learned from Dr. D'Amico to practice video-assisted surgery by just making two incisions."

He then returned to A Coruña and operated using two ports. He practiced the first case with three openings, but only used two to see how it worked. For the next case, he went to the operating room with the head of the department, and explained what he had learned from Doctor D'Amico, and they performed the surgery together. From there, every time the head wanted to practice video-assisted surgery, he asked Diego to accompany him, "in case there was any bleeding or something like that. I was the one who had the training, and little by little, the experience too." However, his boss continued opening up his patients, performing the terrible thoracotomy. Diego gradually modified the technique and in time started using only one of the two ports —and thus one could, in effect, consider April

2009 as the first real Uniportal VATS lobectomy. He kept on opening two but only using one in order to gain experience and to avoid potential problems with his boss. Finally, he and his colleagues did an experimental course with animals, on which they practiced with one single incision, and *voilà*, it can be done!

In June 2010, Diego dared to operate on the first human being through one single port, using only a 4cm utility incision. Previously, he had published a scientific article in the European Journal of Thoracic Surgery in which he described the first 40 cases operated on through two ports, which was in itself ground-breaking in Europe. He had presented it to the Head of Department to read who had decided to claim himself as the primary author, without having written a single letter of the paper, with the three assistant surgeons on his team as secondary authors. "In the end, he was my boss," Diego says now. "Although I would never have done something like that, I wasn't willing to stand up to him for a publication. I thought, as ugly as it was, it wasn't worth the fight."

When he took the step into the first single port operation, it was a very well thought out decision, based on the more than 40 cases in which, despite opening two incisions, they used just one of them. The first operation was filmed. "Beforehand we explained to the patient what we were planning, who accepted, with the caveat that that we would make the second incision at any time, if needed. The operation was fast, comfortable and wonderful. I was excited to tell my boss, but he wasn't working that day, and after that he immediately went on vacation."

A few days later, during which the team continued working, Diego bumped into the Head of Communications of CHUAC, and told her about their success. She said it seemed appropriate to publish it in the press. Diego tried to contact his boss three times but could not locate him. They decided to make their operation public but made sure to attribute it to the team led by the head of the department.

When the Head returned from vacation his first reaction to finding out about the operation wasn't bad. However, something must have crossed his mind, second thoughts or fears, because after two weeks, he called Diego, his assistant physician and said, "This can't happen. You can't work like this." Diego explained to him in detail that it was a logical, well-studied and measured conclusion, and not a spur of the moment decision. But irreversibly, the doctor would begin to feel out of place: he was not the protagonist of the film and so, the punishment began.

The Head of Department gathered the whole team to-gether and instructed them to oppose Diego's pioneering technique. Nevertheless, his colleagues stood up against their boss and declared their support for Diego. They were all so disgusted with the abuse they endured that an assis-tant physician gave up his position and an R-4 quit.

A few days after this meeting, Diego performed a second operation with Uniportal, this time starting and finishing the operation with a single port. His boss found out, and went to complain to the administration, telling them he was practicing a non-prescribed technique. The adminis-tration contacted several international surgeons, includ-ing Doctor D'Amico, to consult them if what was being practiced in the hospital was effectively something dan-gerous or not recommended. "The administration could not decide something like that on their own, they needed scientific and surgical consulting, and so they sought out the most prestigious hospitals. The administration did the appropriate thing, and each and every one of the surgeons consulted responded by saying that what I was practicing was the correct scientific evolution of an oncological surgery that had been evaluated and recognized throughout the world." The administration backed him up, and in the end, he wasn't reprimanded. In retaliation, the Head of Department's reaction was to give his assistant physician the most complex patients and wait in anticipation for a problem to arise in one of the pioneer surgeries. Diego began to enter the operating room gripped with fear of a complication, "because it was what he wanted. If in normal circumstances, you have a problem, it's known that surgery is not an exact science, but at that time, I was operating with a non-prescribed technique, and in such a conflictive atmosphere, the slightest error meant the end of Uniportal, because it would have given him the reason he was looking for. That tension lasted several months, but each patient went slightly better for me. All surgeries were perfect, with two major surgeries per week. It is one of the things I am most proud of in life, of having past the trial by fire."

In October of the same year, Ricardo and Diego had secured their residencies after passing their exams and had begun to head down the promising path that had opened with this new technique. It was the same path that the Chief hoped to block. Along with Mercedes, they decided to open a private clinic in order to be able to operate calmly without any pressure, and especially in order to be able to advance and evolve the technique. From there, the Minimally Invasive Thoracic Surgery Unit (UCTMI) was born. That was when the Head of Service went "into a total tailspin."

He declared an all-out war on the three, because he considered Ricardo and Mercedes to have betrayed him. "I felt so supported by them, by the entire service, and the entire hospital...Everyone thought that what the Head of Department was doing was an outrage," an outrage in terms of the evolution of science. However, going to work became hell for them; the chief made their lives impossible. Diego will never forget the dishonor of the day a surgeon came from Madrid to see how they practiced video-assisted surgery. It was a tumor they had decided to operate on through two ports because at that time, not all cases seemed to be candidates for Uniportal. The Head of Department showed up in the operating room in the middle of the surgery, and Diego told him not to wash up, it wouldn't be necessary, everything was going well; but he washed up anyway, and approached the operating table, and without further ado, he made an additional cut in the patient. "It's for your own good," he said, "And he started to insert tools through the incision, to bother me and to show his authority. It was Dante-esque. The surgeon from Madrid was shocked, it was such a lack of respect." The Head of Department was causing pain and assaulting the patient, just to oppose his crusade. "I felt as if he had violated me, because he also did it so naturally and coolly, without uttering a word: that was him."

In that same year of 2011, Diego's colleagues, assistant physicians Mercedes de la Torre and Ricardo Fernández sent a very eloquent letter to the CHUAC management, in which they reported, "...the obvious professional assault directed toward Dr. González Rivas, which secondarily affects the other members of the service, because it generates great tension. It is a flagrant situation of workplace bullying that scares us and destabilizes us physically and must stop once and for all." The clinical sessions turned into just that, a real hell. "On the battlefield, he moved like a fish in water, he was used to it. But I couldn't sleep. In my life, I had never been in a fight or anything like it." Diego endured so much pressure that year, that in 2014 he separated from his partner, the great love of his life. He took refuge in his work, and in the compassion and support from his closest friends and family. This great obstacle in his life transformed into an engine that drove him to overcome any challenge. From there, his global crusade for Uniportal VATS began, in which he undertook an endless journey to demonstrate the viability of the technique to the world.

***

Alienation: that is how Diego summarizes those years, which threatened to last too long. "The Chief spent all of his time looking for something to accuse us of. He accused us of any little thing, time and time again. It was him against the world, while we were dedicated to working. He changed our surgical indications, he scheduled cases of open thoracotomy that we refused to do, he would cancel our operations, day after day, until a time came when I couldn't take any more and I rebelled, sick of it. I went to his office to ask him why he required all of that from us, and he violently threw me out of the room. He grabbed me, but I stayed still. He started to shake me, and he pushed me against the door frame and closed it on my face. He fractured my nose from the blow of the door. I waited a full day for him to say sorry, but when I didn't receive the slightest apology, I reported him. All of my colleagues spoke in my favor, of course, because they had seen it, it was so obvious... And so they ordered him to compensate me for damages."

Three days after issuing the ruling, the Head of Service started up a defamatory press campaign. However, at the same time, the hospital had begun to see that the conflict had turned the service into a rudderless ship and ordered an audit to be carried out. This was in 2012. The Sergas inspectors investigated and discovered endless irregularities in the management of the service, in addition to the existence of the private foundation to which they were going to stop all deposits and contributions from laboratories for the development of the public thoracic surgery service. They decided to fire him, protected by the fact that he had never even passed the specialized training for his position, he had just been chosen somewhat at random. However, they committed an administrative error in processing the termination, because they didn't provide the 15 days of prior notice, instead the hospital management made his dismissal effective immediately. Mercedes de la Torre assumed the management on an interim basis. "We felt tremendous relief, he became just another assistant. But he wouldn't leave it at that. His lawyers dug up the administrative error and won the lawsuit, so it was required that he be reinstated in August 2013. His defamatory campaign blew up in the press, spreading true panic among society regarding Juan Canalejo thoracic surgery. He argued that the technique we were applying was dangerous, and was not clinically tested," and claimed that they unfairly sent patients to their private unit.

At that time, the technique had already started to expand globally, and in the surgery department, they had scheduled a series of international courses with great impact and success, that were broadcast to the entire world. In one of the courses, a patient suffered a post-operation complication that the Head of Department (which he was once more) didn't hesitate to use to attack Doctor González Rivas and his team again in one of the most widely read daily newspapers in the country. He accused them of inappropriately operating on the patients, using unauthorized instruments, and again underscored the dangerousness of the technique, etcetera. The assistant surgeons in the Medical College investigated the attack campaign, and a detailed report was created. As a result, the Chief was fined, and proceedings were filed to the professional institution for leaking confidential data to the press.

Nevertheless, hospital management had been forced by judicial ruling to reaccept him, so they had gone back to being in hell. Despite the administration watching over the conflictive boss, he had gone back to conspiring from within the service he was again directing. One morning, he decided to personally operate on one of the patients that Diego had scheduled for Uniportal. He was going to perform the surgery, and he was going to do it by performing an open thoracotomy. The patient, a young man, begged him not to do it, but the stubborn surgeon went down to the operating room and opened him up brutally from top to bottom, unnecessarily and against his will. The patient reported his "outrage" about what had happened, but unfortunately, it wasn't the last episode. Shortly thereafter, the Chief refused to let Uniportal VATS be practiced on a colleague, the Head of Department of Urology of the Jove University Hospital in Oviedo, who was suffering from lung cancer. The colleague had undergone all the preparations so that a pulmonary node could be operated on at Juan Canalejo Hospital by Uniportal, but again, out of spite, the Chief prohibited the operation unless it was he who practiced an open thoracotomy. In the end, Diego was forced to operate on his esteemed colleague in his private unit, which he refused to charge for, obviously. The colleague wrote one letter to the CHUAC administration, reporting what had occurred, and another directly to the Chief in which he expressed, "my most vehement condemnation for your lack of ethics and service, which our code of ethics requires you to have for me as a patient as well as for me as a peer."

More letters surfaced from patients that were subjected to unnecessary open surgeries that were solely motivated by professional jealousy and hate. In December 2014, the administration dismissed the doctor again as Head of Department, this time taking care to not make any mistakes in the proceedings. At that time, the dismissed person took a leave of absence for depression (waiting to retire in April 2016), to better develop his Machiavellian strategy. He masked his personal and dreadful battle by creating an association under the pretentious name, White Coats (Batas Blancas), a sibylline parapet to go against Diego and against the public institution that refused to support him. He mustered up a few colleagues who were furious and resentful against Servizo Galego de Saúde, to whom he presented a ploy to carry out his sole objective: to sink the CHUAC thoracic surgery service. "I won't stop until I destroy the service and finish off Uniportal!" were the exact, eloquent words of the Chief to Doctor De la Torre (his replacement on the job).

In his next rampage, he would accuse them of diverting patients from Public Health to their private unit. He compiled the history of a series of patients who were operated on in the UCTMI in order to avoid the waiting lists that would make their cases non-operable or fatal (such as the case of the teacher Ana Briz, which we'll discuss later on) or simply because the surgical team corresponding to the public service did not consider their tumors operable (such as the case of Carmen López, Joaquín Silva and so many others). On top of that, even more complaints and negative articles were written by sympathetic journalists in various media outlets. The judge investigated, interviewed each and every one of the patients individually. "Despite being innocent, it was very hard to be immersed in a baseless judicial process and be attacked in such a way in the press. Although I must say, our prestige was not affected whatsoever, and fortunately, most people understood the personal motives of the accusations. But before that, I had never had enemies; it was something completely foreign to me." It was an unsuspected and late discovery for a kid who had freely offered his generosity.

It was also a great learning experience that he wants to share, "Don't become disillusioned when others refuse to help you, when they try to stop your progress. Remember in those times the words of Albert Einstein, "I feel enormous gratitude to all those who told me no. It's because of them, I did it myself."

PART TWO: JOURNEYS

CHAPTER 9:
Uniportal in Real Time

*The patients scrutinize everything. They interpret your gestures
and words in ways that you cannot even imagine; they worry
that you will hide even the smallest detail from them.*

Things like this rarely happen to other people, but for Diego they are a) understandable and b) characteristic. It's early July, and he has just arrived from Shanghai where he has been giving courses. He made the most of his 12 days in China by doing operations in the cities of Weihai, Hefei and Huan'an (all "very complicated cases," he said). On his flight back from east Asia, he stops in Girona, Spain, where despite his jet lag, he meets with the Spanish Surgeons Circle at a seminar titled: Innovation in Surgery. In Spain, he spends just four days in A Coruña, but not to rest —it seems as if the word doesn't exist in his vocabulary. At home, he rises with the sun and paddles out into the ocean that he knows best. At sunrise and sunset, he rides the crests of the waves. The rest of the time he's on call for his obligatory shift at the public hospital, and he also attends to patients arriving from the most unlikely parts of the world to be operated on by his hands.

At the end of the four days, having completed the final operation, he returns home at night after an unusually hot day in the Galician city. He has to pack for his next tour of duty: he is to leave early tomorrow morning for a nine-day trip to Latin America to participate in several conferences and give Uniportal VATS master classes in Chile, Brazil, Peru, Bolivia and Mexico. His shirt sticks to his skin from the thick humidity that on hot days evaporates from the estuary. He opens his closet and takes out a lightweight Merino suit, some dress shirts, and some T-shirts and jeans for walking around the warm Southern Cone.

He leaves home at 8:00 a.m., and after a layover in Madrid, he reaches Santiago, Chile the next morning wearing his typical outfit: white shirt with a surfer logo and jeans. As the plane starts to descend toward Santiago, Diego is surprised to see the snowy peaks out the window, just as the pilot announces, "Ladies and gentlemen, in 30 minutes we'll arrive to the Santiago-Pudahuel airport, where the temperature is zero degrees Celsius. The skies are cloudy, and..."

So, there is Diego: hanging out in the Santiago, Chile airport in short sleeves amongst a sea of people up to their eyebrows in winter coats and scarves. "It didn't occur to me that of course, it would be winter here! Southern hemisphere! And Chile is a country of very extreme weather. It didn't even cross my mind. I was thinking tropical temperatures, and as it turned out, they had to lend me a coat and several sweaters, because this city is freezing. What an oversight!" he laughs in the voice message he sends from the other side of the world.

***

Four months earlier, in early March, we were having one of our face-to-face interviews in front of the beach of Riazor, A Coruña. At midday, a bountiful family Sunday lunch would be waiting for Diego at his parents' house to celebrate his fleeting visit after two months of international travels, from corner to corner of the globe, from Tibet to Havana, passing through the Middle East, and the cold northern part of Europe. His mother has prepared her specialty —rice with lobster— as well as an oven-baked apple pastry, which they enjoyed over delicious coffee and post-lunch conversation at the table. The coffee flowed, as did the stories of Diego as a child; some of which his parents and aunts will share later; other stories we imagine will remain private, for the family alone.

By Tuesday, Diego was back in the air, this time heading via Madrid and Frankfurt to the capital of Slovenia. Once in Ljubljana, he decided to treat himself to a good dose of adrenaline in order to recharge his batteries, because after that, he had another two months of circling the globe without respite, bringing Uniportal VATS to the most unexpected places. He had arranged to meet the surgeon, Tomaz Stupnik, the driving force behind his single port technique in Eastern Europe, and the organizer of the conference he was attending in the neighboring Croatian city of Split. They had not arranged to meet in a 'normal' place, but rather in a heliport on the outskirts of the Slovenian city. In addition to being a thoracic surgeon, his friend is a pilot of engineless planes. These are the kinds of things that happen to Diego, and as the old saying goes, 'Birds of a feather flock together.' In order to take off, airport personnel push the end of the wings of the plane until "it's flying!" Diego posts a video of his fantastic journey above the snowy peaks of the Julian Alps and Lake Bled on his YouTube channel (videocirugiatoracica, which has more than 2,000 surgeon subscribers). In the film, you can only hear the sound of the wind, interspersed with expressions of awe and wonder. Amazing! The flight and beaming faces are truly incredible; the added touch of Diego's plaid fedora makes the whole thing appear as if straight out of a scene from *Monsieur Hulot's Holiday* with Monsieur Hulot saun-tering along the beach.

They land, and the next day, Diego will meet with his anesthesiologist, César Bonome (also known as 'the man of your dreams,' as he sometimes introduces himself to his patients). He has also come for the course scheduled in Croatia. Together, they will successfully perform a live case of right upper lobectomy at Split University Hospital on a lung cancer patient, broadcast in real time for teaching purposes. It ends up being a curative surgery, yet again, which in colloquial terms translates into a successfully re-moved cancer.

After a quick stroll around the historic city at sunset, an early morning flight via several layovers will bring Die-go to Taipei, where the 4th Asian Conference of Uniportal VATS is taking place: 463 surgeons are registered from all over the world, representing some 20 nationalities. It had been an annual conference in Asia for the last four years. Prior to this, it was held in Hong Kong twice, and once in Seoul. This year, the conference is held in the capital of Taiwan, organized by National Taiwan University Hospi-tal. The organizers set the pace: two days of hectic activity.

The Taiwanese are global pioneers in tubeless thoracic surgery, and so in the surgery on the last day of the sympo-sium, the patient is breathing naturally without assistance (non- intubated technique). It isn't, as one would expect, a simple surgery: the tumor presents complicated adhesions on the upper lobe of the left lung. Another not-so-insignificant fact is that the operation is broadcast live online throughout Asia. Diego has several expert anesthesiologists, and a total of 10 people in the operating room, but it is he who handles the instruments, acts and operates. The patient responds well to the operation, and the results are very satisfactory. "It went great" says Diego, who ends the day "wiped out." Afterward, he goes out to eat with the team of surgeons. The next day is Sunday, and for once, he has the day off.

Free, but scheduled —Eastern-style. When colleagues don't accompany him on the excursions, as usually occurs in the East, the organizers of the courses (in the East, they barely understand the term 'leisure') send him chaperones and so Diego sends funny pictures, surrounded by women on his visit to the Upside Down House —a home built by a group of architects in the recreational park of Huashan that gives you the sense of being upside down: you walk with your feet on the ground, but everything except your hair and your arms resists gravity, from the car in the garage to the bed sheets. In the afternoon, he has enough time to swim for a few hours: the water is Diego's natural habitat, where he relaxes. Later that night, he joins the surgeon Gaetano Rocco for dinner. The Italian is a pioneer of the single port concept applied to minor surgeries. They dine at the restaurant Din Tai Fung, the only Taiwanese restaurant with a Michelin star.

Relaxed after a good meal, Diego goes home to bed: his flight is to depart early the next morning. This time, he is headed to Osaka, where he will participate in the 116th

National Surgery Conference of Japan. It features 10,000 surgeons, including Japanese and foreigners. There, Doctor González Rivas will give several talks about Uniportal VATS before a notable audience (notable not just in numbers).

He lands one day before the conference; in his personal journey dedicated to science he is always alone, yet always accompanied. He takes advantage of the day to visit Kyoto and its wonderful gardens, Buddhist temples, Shinto sanctuaries and enormous imperial palaces. He gushes over the experience, "I am truly lucky to be able to visit this city in the full splendor of the cherry trees blossoming." You can see them everywhere on the beautiful landscape and on the women's festive kimonos. Later, he has the pleasure of eating at the "best Japanese restaurant ever." It is a modest place, full of locals, and "absolutely incredible." Such are the tiny yet paradoxically huge moments of pleasure that Diego enjoys to the last detail.

Osaka is springing with surprises for the surgeon. The first is that he is informed that there had been an earthquake the day before. The second is a call from one of his recent patients in Spain, Carmen López —the case we opened this story with. Doctor González had recommended not doing a check with a CAT scan until six months after the surgery. "...because the inflammation that is underlying the operated area sends false images, which tend to be false positives." However, her oncological team had given in to pressure from Carmen: she wanted to know, and could not contain her anxiety any longer, so she had undergone the test.

The reason for her anxiety was due to misgivings that had persisted since the post-operation appointment. She had not told anybody about them, not even her husband; however deep in her soul she was afraid that something was not right. Doctor González Rivas knows how to look into a patient's eyes and explain the situation clearly and directly, "Although later they interpret gestures and words that you cannot even imagine; the patients scrutinize everything. They worry that you'll hide the smallest detail from them. Sometimes, they are so mistrustful or so anxious that when I tell them they must receive a preventative chemotherapy session after the operation, to them, it sounds like, 'Oh, something is going poorly, and he's not telling me.' But no, it is only because it is recommended to prevent recurrences."

When Carmen had gone to the post-operation review, the pathological anatomy report of the tumor (the much-feared Rusca, now lifeless and in formalin) was not ready. "Then Diego had a conversation with the pathologist that raised some questions for me," says Carmen, "because I detected silences, and some of what he said was imperceptible, like a coded message, but then afterwards he spoke so that I would hear him." Half an hour later, they brought the report, and Diego gave her the all-clear. "I left the consulting room more than radiant on that unforgettable January 5th." The doctor had likely been complaining *sotto voce* about the delay in producing the aforementioned report, even though it was in the middle of Christmas vacations. Nevertheless, Carmen's misgivings remained deep inside, so deep that she didn't even confess them to her husband. She now says that this was the impetus of her insistence to the oncologist: she needed to know, one way or another. Three months after the operation, she had an un-recommended CAT scan.

***

She received the results that afternoon: there is an up-take (that is, abnormal glucose absorption, which denotes cancerous tissue) near to the same place where the tumor was previously removed along with the entire lobe as a means of preventing the spread of malignant cells scattered around the area, previously treated with chemotherapy and radiotherapy. Diego can't understand the report, and he requests Carmen's husband to immediately send him the images of the CAT scan. Once Diego has the images he provides his feedback instantly. It is 5 o'clock in the afternoon in Ourense, and 2 a.m. in Japan, yet Diego answers a Skype call from Carmen and her husband at the same time as he opens the email with the CAT scan images. Right away, he establishes calm: he is nearly sure it is a false positive. "But I have to see the images from before the operation (which are in his office in A Coruña) and compare the two." In addition, these new images cannot be seen clearly on his cell phone, and he isn't able to draw conclusions. Still, he manages to calm the patient down: either it's a false positive (which normally happens due to inflammation and leftovers from anti-coagulants that are left in the internal wound) or it is an unprecedented case. He sets her up for a visit with his team at the UCTMI in A Coruña. He will see her there as soon as he returns (in one month). The oncological team serving Carmen follows the surgeon's exact instructions and repeats the test three months later. In the meantime, they advise her to try to breathe normally. Carmen keeps on trusting Diego, and that night she is able to sleep like the calm after the storm.

At the prescribed time, six months after the operation, Carmen undergoes a new CAT scan which gives the results predicted by the surgeon: the uptake had reduced to half of its size, and the shadows of the metastasis in the liver (which has also erroneously thrown off the test) has disappeared. He concludes —much to their assurance and joy— that it was a false positive and the surgical recovery would continue its normal course. Carmen is revived for a second time. Diego is the hero, and Carmen can continue to take baby steps, without making too much noise, lest she awaken the shadow of the terrifying Rusca.

***

A third surprise is awaiting Diego that night in Osaka. In the early morning hours, a dream shakes him from his sleep. But is it a dream or is it happening in real life? He is dreaming about the earthquake that shook the city on the night before his arrival, but is he just dreaming or is the tremor shaking his bed real? He wakes up; indeed, everything around him is moving. Startled, he gets out of bed. Diego, that small but great man who knows no fear, is actually scared for once. He doesn't have the slightest idea of what to do when something like this happens, because what is happening is an earthquake. There are a few seconds of fear, and he hears voices, which he follows into the hallway. From there, he discovers that all of the guests have done the same. They too have jumped out of their moving beds and are huddling in the hallway. "We were all looking at each other with the same question on our faces: what do we do? Suddenly, a hotel employee appeared and calmed us down. He said it was passing, and to remain calm." And keep calm he does. "Those who weren't tourists were calm and said there was no danger. They were used to the tremors and knew how to distinguish them." He returns to his room and records the aftershocks of the earthquake with his cell phone camera: click-clack-clunk. After an hour, he goes back to sleep. He has little time remaining before setting out again, this time to Shanghai, which today is like his second home in the world. Beep-beep. It is 4:50 a.m. in Spain and a text message appears on the phones of his friends, colleagues and family. Tomorrow they'll see the news about the earthquake in Osaka. Diego sends them a message from the boarding gate. This is his life, as told by him.

CHAPTER 10:
Shanghai Connection

When it comes to fighting cancer, we're all the same:
Keep calm and think Uniportal!

His great friend and collaborator in Asia, Tim, receives him at the airport. He's a thoracic surgeon, 30 years-old, and looks like a kid with his short stature and beaming face. He's a local celebrity, yet after seeing him in the documentaries that Diego's team has filmed in east Asia, one cannot imagine him as anything but a youth. His real name in Chinese is Yang-Yang; however, he westernized his name to Tim Young to make handling international work easier. "He's like my little brother in Asia. We always travel and operate together whenever we can."

It is Sunday, on the eve of the second international training at the Shanghai Pulmonary Hospital, and Diego and Tim enjoy a free day. What better way to do so than the Formula 1 circuit: speed is a passion they both share. They go to the race, and someone mentions to them that that night, the drivers and their teams will be having a party at Mint, the coolest and most glamorous night club in the Chinese metropolis, and of course —*of course*— they are invited. Wherever they go, they are guests of honor. Like any other kid, Tim is dying to meet Fernando Alonso. After Diego does a few laps in the pool, they have dinner and head to Mint together. There, they find the Spanish driver, who gives them a friendly greeting and shows interest in Diego's progress in thoracic surgery. "I found him really up-to-date on the topic. Perhaps it has something to do with the collapsed lung he suffered during training at Montmeló, but he was really informed." He takes a selfie, and posts it on Facebook, and then goes straight to bed: he has a tough week ahead of him.

**

As usual when this bi-monthly training is held, the 18 thoracic surgeons are amongst the most distinguished in the world. On this occasion, they come from Brazil, Spain, South Africa, Egypt, Colombia, Russia, Peru, Austria and Lithuania; 12 simultaneous operating rooms and an average of between 40 and 50 operations per day. He personally carries out 3-5 operations each day, surrounded by a team of no more than 8 people, while the trainers rotate from table to table in the operating room. The days start at 8:30 a.m. and doesn't end until night. That day, more than 3,000 surgeons from around the world will connect to see the 10 surgeries they are broadcasting live from the Shanghai Pulmonary Hospital; 10 of the 45 total cases operated throughout the day.

Later that week on Friday, the course organizers gift everyone tickets to the Beijing Opera. "It's supposed to be amazing —and I'm sure it is but I was so exhausted that I was falling asleep during the show. Plus, for three straight hours I couldn't understand anything. Not a word, no subtitles, nothing! It was really Chinese!" His observations give some perspective: he is in an area where until 30 years ago, not a single tourist, business person or foreign professional had ever been seen. At least he is able to rest in his seat at the opera, because after he leaves the show, Diego has another long trip ahead: a journey to Changzhou, a three-hour drive northwest of Shanghai.

***

"Warm welcome for Professor González to visit Changzhou Number 2 People's Hospital," says the neon signs welcoming Doctor Diego to the entrance hall of the mega hospital of this Chinese megalopolis with a population of five million residents. It is part of the prosperous province of the Yangtze Delta, which has a population of nearly 40 million citizens. Two patients are waiting in the operating room, as well as a team of 10 surgeons who want to perfect the Uniportal VATS technique in order to later practice and continue disseminating it.

However, the day isn't finished yet. It is Saturday afternoon, and the astronomical traffic ahead of him clogs the region's saturated highways: the three-hour one-way journey in the middle of the night turns into five that afternoon on his way back to the Shanghai airport. Of course, that means missing his flight that was to take him to Weihai, a seaside city farther to the north, on the coast of the Yellow Sea, in front of the Korean shoreline. Instead, he takes the next flight, and when he finally reaches his destination, the top brass of Weihai Municipal Hospital comes to meet him. It is the fourth time that Diego has come to Weihai to teach Uniportal VATS, and as always, they have prepared a generous dinner in his honor, to which the entire thoracic surgery staff and the president of the hospital center are invited. "The worst thing," he says later, "was the *moutai* (declared the national liquor of the People's Republic of China during the Cultural Revolution: a liquor that is obtained from distilled sorghum). In dinners like that, they all drink a lot of moutai, and you have to drink it as well, out of courtesy: rejecting it is an unforgiveable insult." Diego does what he can (pretending to drink).

That night, Diego enjoys a brief and intense sleep in the hotel bed, always the same hotel, in one thousand different cities, the same backdrop of neutral curtains, the tea or coffee set placed on an unappetizing tray, impersonal rooms in impersonal hotels for executives of high standing, and in his case, executives of the operating room. The next day, he has five complicated operations: which are always reserved for the master. At the end of the day, he'll discover that one of those five patients or complex cases, is the Governor of the Shandong province. The province is one of the richest and most successful in China thanks to its crops, industries, diamonds, petroleum and trade with South Korea and Japan. "The Governor's family was very grateful. In order to avoid additional stress, they normally don't inform me of these things before the operation. This is the usual practice in medicine (to not reveal the patient's identity) and, personally, I am thankful for that: when it comes to fighting cancer, we're all the same." Its devastation doesn't differentiate. There is no race, religion, social class, political ideology or sexuality that can save you from its cruelty.

***

That night, he returns to sleep in Shanghai, where he will teach the second part of the course. Dawn breaks at 7:00 a.m., and by 8:00, he is already in the operating room: it is a common schedule in China. That's how he starts his "really difficult week:" three exhausting days of training and a surgery that is broadcast live to a conference in Budapest. On Thursday, he dedicates the morning to doing what they call an 'experimental surgery,' practicing with animals. In the afternoon, he travels by car, some three hours from Shanghai, to the Island of Zhoushan in the southeast, connected to the continent by a 25-mile bridge. There, he operates on another complex case. In the afternoon, he eats dinner at the port, at a fish market at one of the oldest fish centers in the world, and then he returns to Shanghai, where he arrives at one in the morning. Told like this, this trip seems impossible or surreal; it's only possible and real because this is China, and Diego has become Chinese after four years of following the local pace and intensity as he worked up and down the entire country. In fact, he says that in this past operating room, nobody spoke a word of English. 'A number' which has to be clarified with the help of the Chinese that his 'brother,' Tim has taught him. To show how scarce English is in the area, he posts a funny picture online of a small restaurant, at the front of which, there is a large red sign that says, "Fast Foor."

The closing day of the training in the Shanghai Pulmonary Hospital will be in the same vein: an opulent denouement with three "extremely interesting, very difficult and beautiful cases: one sleeve (which is also called a bronchoplasty or bronchial reconstruction in a sleeve); there was also a segmentectomy or removal of a section of a pulmonary lobe, and finally a subxiphoid lobectomy." To understand it, let's read what he wrote for the surgeons who follow him on social media: *"IMPOSSIBLE IS NOTHING! Segmentectomy S3 combined with subxiphoid lobectomy. Always trying to improve and offer the least invasive option for our patients. The single port subxiphoid approach is interesting for bilateral resections, and for selected cases of major surgery that do not require radical lymphadenectomy."*

Like all International Uniportal VATS Training Courses that Diego González Rivas gives in Shanghai, the event ends with a dinner for the participants at which, instead of diplomas (or in addition to them), white shirts are distributed with a caption in blue letters. Everyone wears them above their shirts for the photo and final toast. On the shirt are the words, *"Keep calm and think Uniportal!"*

CHAPTER 11:
The Case of Eugène Abdullin

I tell him my progress via text message,
and I follow him on Facebook.
For me, he's a genius and a magician:
I haven't had any more problems with my lungs.

Eugène Abdullin is a freelance English teacher in the Russian Republic of Tatarstan, in the city of Kazan, on the shore of the Volga River. As a child, a congenital tumor was discovered on his lung. Although it was benign, it was recommended to be operated on because it was sure to grow, and severe complications could occur. His mother, a pediatrician, refused to subject her child to an open thoracotomy because she was afraid he wouldn't survive it given the aggressive way such an operation was practiced at the time in the Soviet Union (this was in the middle of the Perestroika movement). The operation was also practiced in the same way in the rest of the world, and as we mentioned earlier, continues to be practiced today.

He lived for years without complications. He played sports, took care of himself, and led a very healthy life. However, in 2009, he began to suffer from persistent asthma and continuous episodes of pneumonia. The malformation, located in segment 6 of the left lung, was growing. It grew until it started causing him chronic pneumonia that prevented him from leading a normal life. It forced him to be nearly permanently medicated with strong antibiotics.

"Each passing year was worse for me," Eugène says from his room one Sunday morning, in the early dawn light, his bed still unmade and his work waiting for him in the room. "I had to do something, so I started to gather information about possible solutions. I went to visit the clinic of a doctor in Saint Petersburg who practiced video-assisted thoracic surgery through three ports. The idea of an open thoracotomy terrified me; the mere thought was like a ghost returning from my childhood, causing a blind panic. The doctor advised that I remove the entire lung, and that couldn't be done by video-assisted surgery. According to him, it was anatomically impossible (later, we'll find out removing a lung, piece by piece, isn't impossible for Diego). Coincidentally, the doctor had a Spanish colleague who was visiting Saint Petersburg to teach a revolutionary technique, and even more curiously, this colleague would be traveling to Kazan to give a master class, 'But it's not going to be possible to operate on you there!' warned the doctor, adding yet another impossibility. He gave me the name of this Spanish colleague, and I immediately started to look up Doctor González online. It was easy to contact him. On Facebook, he had a phone number, which I called, and he answered personally! The first response he gave to my questions was, 'Come. I'll solve your problem.' I started to save money up for the trip to Spain, accommodation and operation, and when I had enough, I got back in touch with him, and he gave me an appointment for an operation on July 2, 2015."

It took three hours of video-assisted surgery to remove segment 6 from the left lung through an incision that has left barely an inch-long scar. However, the complicated part was the dissection of the fibrosis that the malformation had left in the fissure, artery and bronchus. It was an uncommon, and therefore, extremely complicated operation, to treat a disease that ostensibly only one in a million people suffer from, according to Eugène. For him, the surgery left no trace on his lung, which when seen with X-rays is a perfectly normal organ. "I've gone back to doing sports, two hours of exercise per day. I breathe without a problem, and I lead a healthy life," says the lively looking 37-year-old man.

Eugène is not just another case for Diego —none of his patients are. During his two weeks in A Coruña, Diego visited him every day. When the time came to say good-bye, Diego took him in his own car to the airport and even carried his suitcase. Upon his return to Kazan, a new life was waiting for Professor Abdullin, Doctor of Philology, Specialist in English and Arabic, three times married and divorced, son of a neo-natal pediatrician and a now-retired computer scientist.

"When I made the decision to be operated on, my wife at the time did not support me. She said I could live for many years with the tumor, and that the operation and what it entailed was very expensive for our budget. My monthly stipend was around 2,000 euros. There is a lot of competition for my work as a freelance teacher, and therefore, I must always be ready, at any time of day. I cannot even allow myself to be sick. So, imagine how my life was with the health problems I had. To boot, at that time, the Russian ruble was really weak against the euro, so I had to work very hard during the entire year to save money and borrow some from relatives and friends. I felt so betrayed by her that I asked for a divorce, 'You can't be my wife any more, I told her.'"

He eventually did go to Spain, spent three days in the hospital, and a total of two weeks in A Coruña, staying in a room he had rented online, in the house of a family that spoke English. He was cared for by Diego at all times, whom he is still in touch with. "I tell him about my progress via text message, and I follow him on Facebook. For me, he's a genius and a magician. That's why I always call him Doctor Genius. Nobody in my country is capable of doing what he did, and even though he comes to Russia often to teach his technique, there is still no surgeon of his caliber, or even close to it. I haven't had any more problems with my lungs."

Abdullin now shares his life with a 21-year-old girlfriend. "I feel like a young man again, without always catching my breath, so I prefer the woman to be younger too." They just got back from summer vacations in the Dead Sea in Jordan, revived.

CHAPTER 12:
Australia: Water and Reflection

One day you're the happiest person in the world, or you think you're God, and the next day, you wake up with a terminal illness or a car runs you over; so, never look down on anybody.

We left the Uniportal VATS journey in Shanghai, at the close of the bi-monthly training Diego was giving to the international community. That Friday night, wearing the KCTU (Keep Calm and Think Uniportal) shirt, he attended the dinner and cocktail party, after which, he slept like a log before it was time to fly again! Next stop, Australia, where he arrives feeling miserably sick. After several flights (Shanghai-Sydney-Brisbane), he reaches his destination on Sunday afternoon to participate in the Royal Australasian Congress of Surgery. He has the 'flu,' or what in any other human being would have been called fatigue or total exhaustion. However, Diego doesn't accept frailty easily, so he diagnoses himself with the flu, despite that being not quite the truth.

The next morning, after having slept eight straight hours (an accomplishment for him), he now has a well-deserved day of sightseeing ahead of him (the conference doesn't start until the following day). For him, the best views are from the sky, so along with the inseparable Tim, he hires a helicopter tour (this time flying with an engine, without acrobatics, in order to accommodate his dear Tim) which will fly over the city and surrounding areas, to the north of Sydney, and tour the Gold Coast. Once they land, ko-alas, kangaroos, pelicans and all types of attractions from the southern city amaze his 'little brother' Tim. To please him, Diego organizes that they have dinner in a Spanish restaurant where anything having to do with Spanish food is pure coincidence. "At least they had Estrella de Galicia beer. That much was real!" Both the blonde beer and the surgeon hail from A Coruña.

The clock strikes 6 o'clock in the morning, and just one hour later, Diego is at the podium, giving a 60-minute mas-ter class in front of Australian surgeons. By noon, he has given two half-hour lectures. The western winds are blow-ing; this time, there are no practical cases or ill-timed trips and operations, for example, to visit a remote community in the middle of the desert and continent. No, this time there will be no surprises. Diego is saving the surprise for himself. He is near one of the greatest surf paradises, which he had already visited in 2000, with the excuse of attend-ing the Olympics with a friend. On that previous trip, they had toured the 2,500 miles of the southern perimeter with a van loaded up with surf boards. Now, on his free day be-fore the closing dinner of the Royal Australian Congress, he thinks, "what are another 120 miles?" A mere jaunt, practically nothing; so insignificant, he doesn't think twice —he is definitely going to seek out the waves at Snapper Rock. "It's one of the top surf spots in the world!"

A surgeon colleague lends him his board, and he finds a driver to take him. In a heartbeat he is zipped up in a thin summer wetsuit. Like Poseidon, he paddles out (paddle out is the verb surfers use to refer to how they get to the line-up —the place where they wait for the wave to break). He spends three hours surfing. "Amazing! This is life!" That's all he can say as he emerges from the water. The driver has to hurry up on the highway on their way back north if Diego is going to make it to the dinner gala and presentation of the diplomas: "Dr. Diego González Rivas. Distinguished Invited Lecturer."

It's one in the morning, southern time zone, and Diego still has time to reflect. Leaning on the pillow of his hotel bed, the same impersonal hotel as always, still dressed in his white shirt from the gala, he connects to Skype. "I wonder why I am treated so well in such a far flung place like Australia" (referring to his celebrity treatment, even though he's only 41-years-old). "Why does my technique have so much impact around the world? What did I do besides create it? Why have I grown so much? I think it's the method of spreading it: the key to what is happening with Uniportal VATS is in Shanghai. Sure, I created Uniportal, but the important thing has been knowing to get connected with the appropriate people, and having the intuition to say, 'The place to be is Shanghai. I need to join them, work with them.' It's like a Formula One driver who seeks out the best team in the world."

***

"Do you feel like a celebrity or a kind of genius? How do you see yourself?"

"No, I consider myself to be smart enough to know how to create my own path. I know how to learn what is important from each person I meet and disregard what doesn't matter. I have the capacity to filter the good and leave the bad behind. This has to do with my character, and my way of life: I've never spoken poorly of anyone, because I just see the good in each individual. Professionally, I've known to surround myself with the best, from a very young age. I also have a gift with people, which has been very important in spreading this technique."

People ask if Diego has a God-complex given that he gets so much attention and recognition wherever he goes. The mere mention of the observation makes Diego laugh. "Come on! How am I going to consider myself a god? Not at all. I still answer people's phone calls (his personal number is still posted on the Facebook page of the Minimally Invasive Thoracic Surgery Unit). I still respond to everybody. People that have a God-complex do not answer to anybody; they're above it all. Those surgeons have a different attitude with patients. I'll never be able to adopt that attitude because I'm aware that there will always be someone who does things better than me. I hope that the people I'm training end up being much better than I am now. That is important in making history (he pronounces the word 'history' humbly, practically blushing). I know that this will happen, and a time will come when I cannot continue to ride the wave. Believing that you're a god sooner or later ends up taking its toll, because when you are no longer number one, how are you going to feel? Humility is fundamental. I'm aware that what I'm doing is important, but I hope that one day things get even better, and that I can applaud it. Look, in life, one day you're the happiest person in the world, and the next day, you wake up with a terminal illness, or a car runs over you and you end up in a wheelchair. It's something I'm always aware of and is something that I see continually through my work. The lesson I take out of it is to never look down on anybody. It's an attitude that sticks." If he hadn't found it out for himself, his work would have taught him, as it continually exposes the extreme fragility of the human condition.

**

Immediately after the gala at the Royal Australasian Congress, in keeping with the Chinese work ethic, Diego takes a shower, changes out of his dress shirt into a casual T-shirt and heads to the Brisbane airport, where he'll board one of four consecutive flights that will finally bring him back to Europe, via Singapore, Dubai, Frankfurt, and finally, Valencia. 48 hours later, after landing in Valencia, Spain, he is participating in the SECT 2016, the seventh conference of the Spanish Society of Thoracic Surgery. A total of 200 assistants are in the auditorium, attending the surgery broadcast live from Shanghai Pulmonary Hospital, moderated by him from Valencia: they perform two anatomic segmentectomies, obviously, with the Uniportal VATS technique. Dr. Diego González: the squarer of circles, the prodigal son of his homeland.

He is longing to return home; and the next day, Saturday, his wish will be granted, but for only 24 hours. The short time he has is full of family, friends, and waves, as there is no pending case that can be resolved in such a short space of time. Diego quickly writes, "This morning, I woke up to surf in Valcobo —tremendous!" That 'tremendous' probably refers to the waves above seven feet tall in sets of 12, along the coast of A Coruña, on the way to

Finisterre. "I'm like new again!" is again how he expresses himself at the boarding gate. He is on his way to Oslo, via London, where on Monday and Tuesday, he'll perform surgeries to teach the Uniportal VATS technique for the first time in Norway.

He loses his jetlag on the Atlantic waves. He doesn't call it jetlag, referring to it instead as a change of schedule. "What is affecting me is the continuous change of schedules. And I can tell in my state of being that I've become more impatient and irascible, especially in the operating room; more irritable. I've discovered that it has a scientific explanation, and the continuous changes of timetable alter your mood. It doesn't happen with people, I'm still affable and very patient, but when I'm in the operating room, now I want everything to go well and go quickly. I want people to be at my level of skill, and sometimes I find myself repeating to my assistants, 'Come on. Come on' to urge them on. At the beginning, I thought things were obvious to me because I was more of an expert —more experience, more challenges; but now I realize that's not the case." It's just a little murmur going back and forth in his head, that wakes him up, those minutes it takes to figure out where the hell he is waking up that morning, what time it is depends on where, at what latitude he's breathing, and in which world he's living that day. "No, it's not like I lose my temper: that I never do. I never get hysterical if someone on the team makes a little mistake or takes longer than I'd like to complete a task, but I am impatient now with situations that previously on wouldn't have fazed me, and very rarely would have bothered me or made me angry." Come on! Come on!

***

It's now May and Diego González Rivas is lifting the trophy cup like a soccer player in the Champions League. This is Naples, Italy, where the 24th edition of the European Conference of Thoracic Surgery is being held. The team of surgeons that Diego leads, the Asian Team (presented with his Asian colleagues), has won the Master's Cup against America and Europe. The Asian surgeons are first-time champions, with the Galician at the forefront, posing as if it is a sporting competition. In the past, the Americans had always taken home the trophy until the Shanghai team showed up with Diego as their leading scorer, the top goal-scorer in the surgical league against lung diseases.

It's ironic (jokes aside) because barely ten days ago, Doctor González Rivas was chosen as a member of the elite American Association for Thoracic Surgery, the AATS, at a symposium that the American association celebrated in Baltimore. Just two Spanish surgeons have the honor of belonging to this society, and even more extraordinarily, today, Diego is the youngest member of the select international society. "I am very happy," he writes, reporting it. "It is the association with the most global prestige. I was nominated by Doctors D'Amico, Gaetano Rocco and Robert J. Cerfolio, three of the most influential thoracic surgeons internationally. To earn a nomination, a certain number of publications and a notable innovation with a decisive impact on thoracic surgery are required," publications that he writes while killing time in planes and airports.

Planes, like the ones he took last August, to Beijing and back in three days in order to discuss and finalize the founding statements for the constitution of the impending Asian Society of Thoracic Surgery along with Alan Sihoe and the most important thoracic surgeons in Asia. One might wonder what a Galician is doing as a founder of an Asian society, but the answer is quite obvious. "When I started to participate in global conferences, nothing was known in the West about Chinese surgery. I think that my job was important to establish a line of communication between the thoracic surgery that was practiced in east Asia and the western hemisphere. Now the Chinese teams are present in all conferences and competitions. In addition, through publications, the entire world has started to know the volume and quality of their surgery. Asia has started to lead the innovations in the field of thoracic surgery, as we saw at this competition. They are very grateful for my participation, and even though I'm just a mere transmitter, they appreciate my enthusiasm and always have me in mind. The American Association, the oldest in the world, has already been around for one century, whereas the European society was constituted in 1992. I think if we are able to connect and join forces with countries like China, India, Japan, Taiwan, etcetera, we'll be able to achieve an important platform for progress and teaching surgery. It could be the greatest in the world —a treasure." In Asia, Doctor Diego González is a leader, and now they consider him to be more Chinese than Spanish (perhaps because of his work ethic), "you're a 60/40," they tell him, "60% Chinese, 40% Spanish."

In the middle of the month, he goes on a tour around China, already his second home. This time, he visits the precious province of Kunming, and it just so happens to be his birthday (August 12 th). He celebrates his birthday twice. One after another, one dinner after another. He feels spoiled by the generous hospitality, of course, but not too exhausted to attend a conference and master class with a live surgery the next day. It goes well, and he returns within four days, rested because he was able to comfortably sleep on the return flight to Madrid. With barely enough time to say hello and goodbye to his family and prepare his suitcase again, this time he is packing his large suitcase that would be dragged through Africa. And maybe, just maybe, in the final hour of the afternoon, the waves will get just a bit bigger, so he can go out with his friends to the beaches past Sabón.

CHAPTER 13:
Africa: This Is (Real) Life!

The enthusiasm that everyone here has for their work, to impro-ve the lives of others —it's priceless. It means more to me to be here operating on people than in any other place in the world.

The first incident that occurs upon landing in Johannes-burg on August 18th on his way to Pretoria, where he was to give the first classes of this 10-day stint in Africa, is that he discovers that his large suitcase (which for others would be considered tiny —such is his austerity) has not made the plane. It has been lost. However, he barely has time to make a claim. It's 7:00 a.m. in the International O.R. Tam-bo Airport, and at 9:00, the first Wet Lab session awaits him at the Onderstepoort Veterinary Hospital in Pretoria (experimental surgery for educational purposes). The next day, he sends a message, "I never imagined giving a pres-entation at an international conference in jeans and ten-nis shoes," followed by a surprised and embarrassed emoji. After a third and intense presentation and workshop, on Saturday, he departs for Windhoek, the capital of Namibia.

As soon as any self-respecting surfer sets foot on this southeast African paradise, they without a doubt travel to Skeleton Bay. After a five-hour drive from the capital, there's a place where the most impressive barrels in the entire world are formed: two and a half miles of uninterrupted waves. The visit was organized by the Namibian Minister of Health, and therefore an official government car takes him there at full speed through tortuous roads, which seem deadly even to him ("I thought we would be killed!"). They finally arrive at one in the morning, to rest and watch the unreal sunrise. "It's a shame we didn't have more time, and the waves weren't breaking, but at least I can say I went to the spot ('I've been there')." He travels with a local surgeon and the medical representatives of the two international firms that manufacture the specific surgical material for the technique he designed: Marc Moneaux, Belgian, and Raul Eekhout, Dutch, both of whom are regular colleagues on their tours around the most remote places in the world. Together, they rent two quads to explore the sands of the vast desert. After that, Diego gets *his* dose of high-risk activity by skydiving over the spectacular desert of Namibia, the one bordered by Skeleton Bay. "This is life!" is the message he sends later, showing his picture over the desert and ocean, taken from 12 000 feet, the perfect curve of the Earth's silhouette beneath him. It's worth seeing him: jumping from a plane, throwing himself into the open, the surgeon has the face of a child on a carousel at a festival, the tension just before the laugh. It is the human expression of this neuron-shaking hormone called adrenaline.

They sleep in a safari tent. The next day they'll do some exploring before returning on the road to the capital, where at four in the afternoon, the first conference at the Namibia School of Medicine will be held.

The reception at the university is a spectacle of rhythm and color in true African style: a group of seven barefoot women in traditional dress welcome him with a dance. It is the Namibian national welcoming dance; for the first time in its history, the country is going to host a video-assisted thoracoscopic operation. Doctor González's visit is highly anticipated, and this is just the beginning. Later that night, Diego sends a photo of his sumptuous supper: an enormous platter full of sauces and other accompaniments, and in the middle, filets of red meat, which turn out to be antelope. "They're such authentic people. Nothing else in the world compares to Africa," he repeats. During the dinner conversation, news breaks that the staplers needed for the next day's operation still haven't arrived.

The case ahead of him at Windhoek University Hospital will be, as always, extremely complex. It is a lung that has been destroyed by persistent tuberculosis for five years. He practices a right pneumonectomy; that is, piece by piece, he completely removes the totally inactive lung which is full of holes and bleeding. Nothing is possible to preserve due to a massive infection. The next day, the master class is front page news of the local newspaper, *Namibian Sun*. They title it, "Surgical Breakthrough." The article goes on to say, "Yesterday Namibia made history in medicine by hosting and broadcasting live an operation practiced by Doctor Diego González Rivas, a surgeon recognized internationally as a pioneer of a new type of video-assisted lung surgery that is practiced through a single incision."

The State Television station also reports the news and interviews the Namibian surgeon who made Diego's visit possible. Doctor Jones Ngaamwa, who had attended a Uniportal VATS course in Shanghai, explains why the operation that morning, in which he and the best university hospital team had participated, made history in the African country. "Thoracic is one of the most essential of the surgeries," the young doctor says in the television studio, "and Uniportal VATS is its future. Doctor Diego is not only a global pioneer of this technique, but the surgeon is capable of performing surgeries that nobody else can. We were lucky enough to learn his revolutionary technique, in addition to his philosophy, and way of thinking, because as he says, 'Impossible is nothing; everything seems impossible until it has been achieved.'" The local surgeon also speaks in his televised interview about the importance of this technique to tackle one of the most persistent diseases in the country: tuberculosis and the lung destruction that comes along with it. He speaks in particular about the case they had operated on, emphasizing the cost savings (in terms of treatment and hospital stays) that Uniportal VATS entails for a public health system like Namibia's. Doctor Jones Ngaamwa shows the camera the personal dedication that Diego wrote for him in a recently published scientific book about Uniportal VATS. After watching the broadcast, Diego remarks: "The enthusiasm that everyone here has for their work, to improve others' quality of life, and the excitement with which they receive me, it has no price. I carry deep joy inside from that."

***

That afternoon, still buzzing with satisfaction, he lands again in Johannesburg. Between there and Pretoria, he will have four hectic days of master classes and live operations ahead of him. First stop: Sefako Makgato Hospital, in northern Pretoria, in the township of Ga-Rankuwa. At 10:00 a.m., he sends a message: "On the way to operating room, we're starting," and a video that would freeze the blood of even the most even-keeled person: the university hospital is a succession of dark tunnels, a labyrinth of exposed brick hallways, with enormous and entirely visible pipes running overhead. "It's an adventure," Diego says; but he encounters the most unexpected thing at the pre-surgery sinks. One of the surgical assistants is putting on two pairs of gloves. Naturally, Diego asks why he is taking such precautions. "Due to the extremely high incidence of HIV that we have here in South Africa." The surgery assistant's colleague is following the same logic. "But this patient's history doesn't include the virus," Diego refutes him. "Here, you never know. It's impossible to know."

In light of his shocking answer, he also asks for an extra pair of gloves, and remembers the amount of times within the last year that he has operated in South Africa without such precautions. "You'd imagine that this information adds tension to the two cases that in and of themselves are extremely complicated that I have ahead of me today, but whatever: This is Life! It's all for the patients. So, let's do it."

It is 11:00 a.m., and Diego is between operations; by mid-afternoon, he will send the surgery report. The first surgery is an upper left lobectomy, in which they remove an enormous tumor that is firmly stuck to the mediastinum. "It was a very interesting class, and all of the surgeons were very surprised and happy." The second would be even more spectacular: it was a very large tumor —4.5 inches— and it was removed through an incision or subxiphoid approach. Why? To teach something to his colleagues, and to set another challenge. "I had never removed a tumor so large from that subcostal pathway, just above the diaphragm; I don't even think in Shanghai we had ever done anything like that. I think it's a pioneer case in the world. They proposed it to me during the session prior to the surgery and I accepted. Also, it was the first subxiphoid operation practiced in Africa. It is paradoxical that something like that has occurred in a place like this, where you are always afraid there are not enough resources, but it has been a unique case, and I am really happy. It turned out really well. The medical staff was so excited, so enthusiastic. They wear their hearts on their sleeves, and it made me feel really good to come here and collaborate to improve their situation. It means more to me to operate here than in any other place in the world." He edits the video of the operation and posts it on YouTube so that anyone can learn from it.

An even bigger surprise (in the eyes of a Westerner) will greet him at the door of this university medical center. When he had arrived, the first thing that grabbed his attention was the security measures set up at the hospital entrance. They were searched from head to toe, and not just them but the inside of the car they were driving, their luggage, as well as their surgical supplies and personal items. On the way out, they are stopped again, and the search is even more exhaustive, so he finally asks one of the security agents, "Why all of this at a hospital? Is it an anti-terrorism measure? For homeland security? Or what's it about?" It isn't that. "It's because they steal babies and traffic them," responds the officer questioned. "It's something very common, and the most recent kidnapping wasn't long ago. A woman walked out with a newborn, so we've had to increase surveillance measures." Diego relates this while recording himself in front of some wooden sheds seemingly in the middle of nowhere. Those wooden sheds are the patients' rooms in the Makgato Hospital, North of Pretoria.

That night, the scene will change 180 degrees. They go to eat supper in one of those compounds for the rich, in a mall with restaurants and architectural reproductions, like a Shopping Village: franchise of the Western world. It is midnight, and he has been on his feet since 6:00 a.m., yet he doesn't feel tired. "When being tired is worth it, it makes me happy." The next day, they pick him up at 6:30 in the morning to operate and broadcast live two other master cases.

***

It is 7:00 a.m. at the Steve Biko Hospital in Johannesburg. On the operating table, there is a middle-aged man, a former drug addict, with the lower lobe of the right lung totally destroyed. They practice a lobectomy on him that they define as "very complex, extremely complex," to which he adds, "It sapped me of all of my energy." It is rare for Doctor Diego to express something similar, so he must be given credit. However, ahead of him lies a second case; it is again a very complicated lobectomy practiced on an obese woman, with the risk and difficulty that such a condition adds. They have dinner, exhausted, without further comment. Tomorrow at 6:30, Diego and Raul will take their fine surgical instruments to Charlotte Maxeke Academic Hospital, also in Johannesburg, more known in the medical field as Joburg Gen (Johannesburg General Hospital). It is a private center, equipped with the latest technology, located in Sir Lionel and Lady Florence Phillips' old mansion and park. At 7:00 a.m., they are in the operating room, and then they have the rest of the day free to do cultural visits related to medicine. Firstly, they go to have breakfast at the house of a surgeon who collects old surgical material, one of Diego's deepest among many other passions. The surgeon first introduced the ultrasound to South Africa, and he has made a museum in his house located at the entrance of an abandoned gold mine. Diego sends photos of a hundred-year-old X-ray machine, glass oxygen pumps, and syringes, the sight of which would turn your stomach.

In the afternoon, they will have time to tour another museum: Baragwanath —a museum of life. It is the largest traumatology hospital in the world, not just because it uses the latest scientific technology but because it sees cases of unrivalled complexity. The victims of the Soweto township's extremely high level of violence all arrive at the Baragwanath Emergency Room: a daily average of 25 injuries from shootings, stabbings, brawls and assaults of all kinds. The center is set up in the facilities of a former military base from World War II and hosts a total of 3,000 beds distributed in several modules, long rooms made up of bunks that Diego likens to, "As if we were seeing Sarajevo in the middle of the war," the totally seized city of the last European war. "It is a true spectacle that the local surgeons wanted to show me. It is quite chilling to walk around here. It is an unimaginable world, but it is necessary to see." A sign in the hallway says it all, "Carrying weapons of any kind is prohibited." Out of interest they show him an X-ray machine specifically designed to detect diamonds stolen and hidden in the miners' stomachs. They tell him they receive people on medical rotations and students from all over the world to learn to treat types of diseases that rarely occur in the Western world.

Tomorrow is the final day of this African journey. As a cherry on top, Diego receives a gift at the Netcare Montana Hospital in Johannesburg: a young patient, 30 years-old, left lung absolutely obliterated by aspergillomas and two consecutive bouts of tuberculosis. There is absolutely nothing left of that lung to work with, so they remove it. It is a highly-anticipated four-hour surgery and there are many fellows in the operating room. Doctor González Rivas cuts the infected, pierced lung segment by segment, and extracts it in removal bags, which look like condoms. The local surgeons look at one another incredulously. Nobody has ever seen anything like it. The entire surgery is carried out through a minimal and single incision. At a certain point during the operation, one of the locals asks Raul, who has been constant at Diego's side: "Do you know how to eat an elephant?" He replies, "I have no idea." "Piece by piece, just like Doctor Diego is doing with the lung." The final result has a very clean look. He closes the incision with just seven staples, and it is the best-case scenario: the aspergillomas and tuberculosis infection has been removed. After finishing the operation, the same South African surgeon goes over to Raul and says, "It wasn't an elephant. It was a mammoth!" Diego maintains that it was one of the three hardest cases in his surgical life, and it has rendered him utterly exhausted. They have lunch in one the swankiest places in town: The Living Room. It has a terrace overflowing with beautiful women, surrounded by the metropolis's skyscrapers. In another three hours, he'll be on a plane returning to Spain. "This is life and impossible is nothing!" he shouts on the jetway to the plane, with the little strength left in him before surrendering to the extendable seat. When he lands in A Coruña, he goes looking for the waves —the waves of life that he never stops facing and taming.

He finds them at Razo Beach. One and a half hour later, he emerges from the water revitalized, ready for a week of appointments, emergencies and important operations marked on his operating room agenda. Again, it is time to pack his bag: next stop, Cuzco.

CHAPTER 14:
Where Oxygen Is Thin

When I experience a lack of oxygen, I become aware of how tough life is, and how the human being is always adapting wisely.

"How did you come to this? Where did your drive to climb the highest peaks come from?"

"Heights fascinate me, as well as the challenges they pose. I particularly love to climb mountains. It's a way of pushing yourself, surpassing nature's strength. At the top, you can just enjoy the isolation, peace, tranquility, pure air. The mountain is always a mystery."

Diego and Tim have been hiking up the Andes mountains above Machu Picchu. They are about to reach an altitude of 9,800 feet, but they can hardly see anything around them beyond the Citadel of Huayna Picchu or Young Mountain. They are exhausted because in addition to the altitude, the past three days have caught up with them: an international course plus wet labs for 80 surgeons from all corners of the globe, then an untimely wake-up at 4:00 a.m., after a few frugal hours of sleep, followed by the first long journey from Cuzco by car, and later by train and bus. They are about to reach their goal only they can see next to nothing through the mist and low clouds that envelop the Andean mountains. Their guide reassures them that in at most three hours, the sky will open up, and they'll be able to enjoy the entire breathtaking landscape. They will feel like they're flying on top of all creation.

"This is the end of the world. It's like touching the sky," Diego says on the way down. Then he adds, "Two years ago, Mick Jagger closed Machu Picchu to see it by himself. He paid one million dollars, but it didn't clear up. That is the most repeated local anecdote. It teaches that money cannot buy everything, because nature has the final word, just as when facing disease: we're all the same."

As they descend, they are exhausted from the altitude, and are on the verge of having what is known as altitude or mountain sickness. A sherpa has to ascend half of the route from the base to bring water to Tim, who has symptoms of dehydration; they had drunk all of the water they had gone up with, perhaps because of the time they had to wait while waiting for the light to break through. They are on their fourth day in the Andes, and Tim is suffering despite having taken an Acetazolamide-based medication, which prevents cerebral edema, dizziness and headaches, and drinking coca tea (non-alkaline, in tea, jam, powder, candies and many edible derivatives common in the local diet). The descent is quite complicated: the rocks are slippery, and both are low on energy. They have to stop every so often to help Tim in order to prevent him from collapsing.

"Is this fascination with heights a conscious or subconscious desire to experience hypoxia (lack of oxygen in the body)? A way of better understanding the suffering of patients?" He had alluded to something like this when he was talking about the near-death experience he had when he was steamrolled by the force of a giant wave in Mentawai.

"I've never thought about it like that, but it is true that the lack of oxygen is an eye-opener, as is trying to get out of it —how I adapt to the circumstances: testing the limits of the human being. I like to experience a lack of oxygen because it helps me to understand many things in life. It's not like I'm going to go seeking out that experience specifically, but I do like to experience it, yes."

He doesn't seek it out, or maybe he does, if we take note of his epic stories. "When I experience a lack of oxygen, I become aware of how tough life is, and how the human being is always adapting wisely". Let's remember that the ancient Eastern practices of yoga and meditation are based on provoking and controlling hypoxia, which removes tension and balances the mental state.

***

They had arrived at Cuzco four days earlier, where the second edition of a Uniportal VATS course has been organized in collaboration with a Peruvian surgeon. Eighty doctors took part in it. "In Cuzco, we get an added bonus, because it is a magical place. We broadcast an operation live that was being practiced by the Shanghai team. Surgeons came from all over America, Asia and Australia. We dedicated the third day to the experimental operating room. Cuzco is a wonderful place. It's the most enchanting city ever, and it's at 11,400 feet of altitude. It's a unique place. Today I gave six talks in Spanish, although sometimes I didn't know what language I was speaking in (he usually teaches in English). We arrived in the middle of the

Virgin of Nativity festival, with dozens of dance troupes, and ancestral dancers performing in the main square." The local and national press gobbles up the surgeon who has seemingly arrived from the stratosphere, and life goes on. Indeed, life does go on, and as it were, a bomb threat prevents the plane from taking off from Lima on which a veterinarian was to fly from Arequipa to bring all of the experimental laboratory equipment. They finally arrive, after one hour of delay, and make the surgeons' practice possible. "The veterinarian is on the way," he says very early in the morning (in his hemisphere). "We're waiting for him here, at a university in the middle of nowhere. It's a Medical and Dental School, surprisingly quite modern. I'm confident that the experimental course will be held in the end." And that's just what happens. "We held the course in the autopsy room, something unprecedented for me, with portable fans and very scarce resources, which sometimes seemed surreal. But the people were delighted, and that's what counts. It's what makes my job exciting: to see them so interested, grateful and hungry to apply Uniportal VATS."

The day after his ascent to Machu Picchu, the normal course of action would have been to enjoy a day of relaxation somewhere in a latitude as inviting as Cuzco's. However, such an attitude has nothing to do with Doctor González, who had heard talk of the Mountain of Seven Colors, the rainbow of stratified earth of eroded rocks, at an altitude of 17,000 feet. One of the 100 places that, according to *National Geographic*, everyone should visit before they die.

They sleep just three hours after the exhausting day in Machu Picchu, and then take a train and then a bus. When they make it to base camp, there are horse trails ahead of them that lead up 1,600 feet to the summit. The arid landscape reminds him of Tibet, where we have already heard that Diego discovered the ultimate, unadulterated essence of being. Less than a half-mile remains before the summit, but the last 330 feet would be eternal, and almost never happen. "Seriously, I didn't think Tim would be able to summit. Step by step, after three hours, and on that final segment, we rested every 30 feet, going super slow. I wasn't worried about him, but the guide had told me about people who had died trying to reach that wonderful summit, people that come in bad shape, after a night of partying, for example, with the alcohol still pulsing through their blood. He also said that there had been cases in recent months of people who had fallen down a valley, or some kids who went up with beer, and got dehydrated after consuming the alcohol in those circumstances. Today was a tough day," he concludes, exhausted.

The next day, they return to supposed civilization: destination Lima, where in the late afternoon, he would remove a tumor from a relative of a surgeon colleague. The traffic in the Peruvian capital in rush hour is equally convoluted: impossible in an emergency. The hospital sends an ambulance to the airport, which races like a rally car across the city to reach the hospital before the medical staff left the operating rooms.

"Today was adrenaline-inducing. I left Cuzco at 5:00 in the afternoon to give a two-day course that we organized with Doctor Edgar Amorin, Director of the National Institute of Neoplasic Diseases, in Lima, but then a colleague heard about my visit and asked me to operate on his relative." Diego doesn't know how to say no and accepts to perform the surgery, which, by the time he arrives in Lima, will be late in the afternoon. However, the biggest difficulty wouldn't be the surgery, but arriving on time in the Peruvian capital. The journey normally takes two and a half hours by taxi crossing the main thoroughfares of the city. However, Diego's surgeon colleague improvises and is able to send an ambulance to the airport, which races to bring him to the operating room, without him even having time to pick up his luggage. The driver appeared in his medical scrubs at a side door to the airport and drove him to the hospital at top speed, so they arrived in just half-hour. "It was straight out of an action movie, pure adrenaline, passing by the cars. The ambulance was zigzagging, and all of the traffic around us was stopped. But here I am, about to perform surgery," he sends a breathless voice message from the hospital. He also sends a video of the ambulance's sprint through traffic: *veritas veritatis*. The surgeon transported, and the surgery results excellent. It ended at 10.30 p.m. Tomorrow is another no less stressful day: a master class with two live surgeries, which is sure to mean there are new surprises because the local surgeons would never give him a simple case.

***

The next morning, he sends two snapshots: him and each one of the two patients that are waiting for him like someone waiting for God, Godot, Ra, Siddhartha. In the photo, their faces show a tinge of fear, not at all because of how unknown the disease is; on the contrary, their trepidation is predicated on the disease's very prevalence. The towns of Ayacucho have an extremely high incidence of lung cancer. They can't believe they have the luck to have a man come from another hemisphere to remove the monster that has been strangling their ancestors for the longest time. Ancestors who had been suffocated by wood smoke in their unventilated thatched huts, just as they continue to live to this day. And now, this surgeon from another world and the public hospital are offering them surgery.

The two women pose with Diego in a room full of hospital beds. They are wearing housecoats, flower-printed, nearly identical gowns, and their jet-black manes of hair hang down their backs. Fear and incredulity mark their faces. It is the eve of undergoing Diego's surgery and he tries to assuage their fears, "Don't worry, everything will go well." Their skin is infused with the smell of burned wood. He can distinguish that from the other human smells he's grown accustomed to. Behind closed doors, surgeons say that human guts smell even worse than animals'. Some skins and tissues even have a particular scent embedded in them, like this of the fire from the hearth.

One of the two is young, even though her appearance doesn't show it. The second is a middle-aged woman, with a wide and short torso, and a pathology that Diego doesn't discover until it is time to operate on her, before an auditorium packed with surgeons from all over the Americas. "The second woman was a terrible case. It was an extremely difficult case to operate on her with Uniportal VATS. It was a large tumor and a lung blocked by many ganglions stuck to veins and arteries, very difficult to dissect. The patient's anatomy also complicated the video-assisted surgery due to her obesity and short thorax. However, the worst was on the inside. My God, when I entered! It seemed impossible. Despite everything, I kept going, and only on the last step, an artery started to bleed. It bled so much that I had to expand the incision, place in a rib retractor (which entails piercing the ribs) and finish the surgery with her chest open. However, (perhaps due to the care given) her recovery was fast and optimal. For the surgeons, it was a challenge. They were very happy with the master class but are disappointed when something like that happens, but those are the risks of doing it live," says Diego like a rock star. "Yes, I visited the two patients after the operation. They were good, and very relieved." For the patients, it was a miracle of mother earth or the spirits of their ancestors; but in reality, it was science and altruism, not spells, that had given them their lives back.

***

The Andean journey doesn't stop at daybreak. After a couple of flights, he lands in Orlando to participate for the fourth consecutive year in the Duke Masters of Minimally Invasive Thoracic Surgery Course —the most prestigious in its category in the entire world, directed by Professor D'Amico. From the southern United States, he'll complete his umpteenth round-the-world journey and cross the Pacific to land in his second home of Shanghai, China.

PART THREE:
PROPHET ON EARTH

CHAPTER 15:
The Case of Ana Briz

*His bedside manner was just spectacular. He gave me
such hope. His words made everything seem simple...
and after the operation, I felt so good, it felt like a miracle.*

It all started after a student-exchange in Poland. Ana
María Briz is an English teacher at the Martaguisela de O
Barco de Vadeorras Institute in Ourense —the land of slate
mines. One summer, she worked as a chaperone at a camp.
On one of their field trips, they visited the Wieliczka mine,
where in addition to touring the old mine tunnels, she and
several students did a salt therapy treatment in the under-
ground chambers. They say it rehabilitates the respiratory
system, and patients with asthma and other allergies and
lung infections from all over the world do a pilgrimage
there for medical care.

A paradox of life, or simply her fate, but Ana caught a
cold in those caves, which she dragged with her back to O
Barco, into her September classes and all the way to her
daily life, including the Step classes at the gym. Although
she finally recovered from the tiresome illness, every time
she exerted herself thereafter, Ana had an acid reflux that
tasted like salt. "No, this can't be from my stomach," she

told herself. She consulted a doctor and explained, "It's not acidic like from the stomach; it's salty." She became so obsessed that after a few months with persistent heartburn, her doctors performed a thoracic and abdominal radiography, and there they saw it —a stain on the top part of her right lung. They referred her to the oncology unit in the Ourense Public Hospital, the main hospital of the province. A bronchoscopy revealed a terrible result: she had a tumor. In later tests, it would be determined that she was in the initial phase, stage 1. Therefore, it was operable (luckily, or perhaps due to her persistence, it was among the 20% of tumors discovered in time). However, instead of operating on her, they sent her for respiratory rehabilitation. It was August 17th, and she was put on a waiting list of at least two months to have thoracic surgery at the corresponding unit, in the Xeral de Vigo Hospital.

"I was outraged. I wrote complaints to Sergas. Having an operable tumor on the lung is a strange lottery to win. It's unusual to detect them in time, and I especially knew that I would be at risk if it grew and became deadly." In a twist of fate that time sometimes provides, three young surgeons from A Coruña (year 2010) had just opened a private clinic for minimally invasive thoracic surgery 15 days earlier. On a September morning, her husband saw the advertisement from the UCTMI in the local newspaper. They called. "We had nothing to lose, and everything to gain." Diego answered personally. They explained her case and he confidently told them, "Come and see me. I'll explain everything, and I'll give you a solution, and then you can decide what to do from there." They visited him immediately. "The way we were treated was spectacular. He gave me so much hope. His words made it all seem so

158

simple. He lifted me up one thousand percent, because I was so devastated before that." Ana thinks the doctor did not even charge for the consultation.

Ironically, on the same day as their visit with Diego, Xeral Hospital called to tell her that she had a slot in their operating room. "I didn't even take a minute to decide. Diego, Mercedes and Ricardo's manner and confidence were light years ahead of the lack of humanity demonstrated in Vigo. I had to pay for Diego's operation, and the other was free, but if you've got the goods, you have to use them to cure your evils," she told herself. She entered the San Rafael Hospital operating room in A Coruña, to be operated on by Diego, on November 18, the same day that the public hospital had finally given her for her operation (after two months of waiting).

As always, the surgical team included César Bonome, who would also be the man of Ana's dreams. "Those four were the best of the best I've ever known." They removed the tumor through two minimal incisions on the upper and middle lobes of the right lung. "The recovery was incredible. I don't think even my recovery from appendicitis felt better. I felt marvelous, so good it felt like a miracle."

However, the nightmare didn't end there. The time that had passed while waiting would be costly. The stage 1 they had diagnosed in August had propagated, and in a checkup shortly thereafter, they found a metastasis on the lower right lobe. Diego and his team went back to operate on her, this time permanently leaving her without her entire right lung. Ana returned to her classes, which are and have been all this time her salvation.

If the damage caused by the passing of time, wasn't enough, two years later, in 2013, a CAT scan reveals a new station in the left lung, a small node that the oncologists recommend treating with chemotherapy. Diego discards going back in to operate on her and explains. "Ana's tumor behaved in a special way. It was a bronchioloalveolar adenocarcinoma that propagated internally through the air. Because of how big it had grown in the right lung during the wait, some of the cells passed to the left lung and grew over time. But at that point, they were faint, minimal and diffuse wounds, which looked like pneumonia, and so they couldn't be removed. Even more importantly, Ana only has one lung. It was very risky to operate on a single lung, as it could leave her with very little respiratory reserve."

Thus, it is non-operable. The oncologists try one chemotherapy after another on her, and they find a treatment that slows the growth, but destroys her. Despite two and a half years of venomous sessions that they apply every Thursday, she shows up every Friday in class before a gang of teenage students. "That way I didn't have time to think about death. I had a difficult time, but I didn't want that damn alien to do me in, no. I wanted to retire on my own volition, after thirty-plus years dedicated to teaching." Ana is originally from Béjar in Salamanca. She is 59 years-old and came to Valdeorras with her partner after several stints teaching in different parts of Spain. She arrived at Ourense after her previous stay in Gijón.

In the opinion of the oncologists, it could develop into something chronic, but the chemo treatment couldn't be stopped under any circumstance. "I was so devastated that I took up researching it on my own and I discovered that there was a Catalan doctor who was performing ongoing trials, for 'rescue' treatments." She didn't think twice about it and went to the office of Doctor Rosell, in his Oncology

Institute of Quirón. "After never-ending tests, the doctor says 'congratulations.' I didn't know how to take that, but it turned out that my case was clearly suitable for entering one of his molecular biology clinical trials. Yes, there was a treatment, with an ALK kinase tyrosine protein inhibitor, which according to the tests, I react to and is the origin of my tumor. The only sticking point was the very high price, but my oncologists in Ourense were able to get a subsidy from the Galician Public Health Administration for the treatment." And the tumor vanished.

She's been taking that blessed pill for three years, happy to be a guinea pig; happy because you can no longer see any malformation or stain or shadow on her single lung, also because, if one day the treatment stops working, Doctor Rosell told her there are new drugs, which are currently showing improvements in oncology. "I am 100% positive. Everything I've been through has changed my values: every day is the first and last of my life. Now I am much happier than I was before. Helping others has become a priority for me, and I've learned to appreciate love and friendship more. My colleagues tell me so every day when I enter school. How can you be so happy to come to work? How can I not be happy? Within a year, I'll turn 60, and I'm going to retire, and enjoy life even more." Ana has just returned from vacation, and no, she doesn't feel one bit of the so-called post-vacation syndrome that so deeply affects teachers after two months of holiday. She says in mid-September to her students, "none of this business about a syndrome. Forget it!" She has gone back to exercising, replacing the hard Step classes with the lighter Pilates. She walks, always on flat surfaces, lest she overexert her diminished pulmonary capacity. She does periodic tests and takes extreme care with her diet, helped by natural remedies like turmeric and others: everything counts, everything helps to keep her energetic and positive.

Each year, she visits her oncologists in Barcelona to find out about the clinical trial and wish them a good year. She remains in permanent contact with the person she considers having saved her life: a young Galician surgeon whom she loves as if he were family. "Calling or contacting Diego is always like receiving a wave of inspiration," she concludes.

CHAPTER 16:
A Coruña, Finisterrae

"Diego is a very popular character in China; he's like a rock star."
Alan Sihoe, Chief of Thoracic Surgery at the
University of Hong Kong Shenzhen Hospital.

We are in front of the sea again, this time on the peaceful slope of the A Coruña coast, in front of the spectacular limestone of Santa Cristina, where the waters of the Burgo estuary flow and deposit its sediments. Outside, the day is bright and warm. It's the end of May, and interest is growing inside the enormous operating room of the Technological Training Center of the Coruña University Hospital. Nine sedated animals are having operations on their thoracic cavities. It is the experimental surgery seminar of the course directed by Diego González Rivas with the support of the two large international firms that manufacture the instruments for Uniportal VATS.

Five of the masters are alongside him: Thomas D'Amico, Head of Thoracic Surgery and Vice President of Surgery at the Duke Cancer Institute (North Carolina, USA); Alan Sihoe, his counterpart at the HKU Shenzhen University Hospital in Hong Kong; Luis Hernández, Mexican, trained in England, and nowadays assigned to the surgical team at Shanghai Pulmonary; Diego's team –María Delgado and Ricardo Fernández, assistants at the Coruña University Hospital Thoracic Unit. The trainees are surgeons from all over the world. There are up to 16 nationalities among the 20 participants ⊠ from South Africa to Lithuania, El Salvador to Poland, Taiwan to the United Kingdom, Mexico to Germany, Peru, Egypt, Colombia, Belarus, China, Greece and Cuba. Some are enthusiastic residents who have been able to join the training from their respective countries, others are masters in the subject matter and don't want to miss this outstanding surgical course. One example is Juan Carlos Collado, the Director of General and Thoracic Surgery at the National Institute of Oncology and Radiobiology of Cuba. Collado had read about Uniportal VATS and had heard talk of the revolution led by Diego; like a good son of other revolutions, he didn't stop until he had contacted him personally. It's interesting that they were able to connect through his friend, the famous Latin singer-songwriter Pablo Milanés, who had had a kidney transplant at Coruña Hospital (the organ had been donated by his wife, the writer and Galician historian Nancy Pérez). At the post-surgery checkup in A Coruña that autumn, Milanés conveyed a message from his friend, the renowned surgeon of the Caribbean island: he wanted to contact the doctor who led a non-invasive and non-painful surgical technique for lung tumors. Diego was invited to teach in Havana. Collado, a great surgeon in Cuban medicine, has come today to perfect the technique. "The day after Diego operated in Havana, I dared to perform my first operation with Uniportal." His colleagues advised him to start with a more minor operation, but he's not a person to be deterred. "I operated on a complicated tumor, and it turned out great. But I want to improve the technique, I want to know more." Thus, he is here today. He will be the one who tomorrow will best explain the poorly diagnosed case that Diego will operate on and will rebroadcast in real time from the operating room. "Diego has given me a great example to follow, not just to me, but to all surgeons. He has demonstrated that so much pain is neither necessary, nor appropriate. Despite the initial reluctance of the medical establishment, especially thoracic surgeons, today 50% of the thoracoscopic operations in the world are being done with Uniportal VATS. Thanks to him and thanks to the legion of young people that follow him." Those are his words —perhaps the most insightful since we began following this surgical revolution.

However, there were others, such as the statements from the apprehensive Doctor D'Amico —apprehensive like any good American and doctor, of talking to someone from the unspecialized press. To say the name Thomas D'Amico is like saying the godfather of the revolution. It was from him that Diego learned the path that led directly to Uniportal, as is told in Chapter Four. However, it's better to let the American master say it in his own calm words, as he opens up to me in the waiting room, after a hospital lunch (tomato and tuna pasta salad, baked hake and apple pudding).

"The first time Diego came as an invitee to Duke, he was with us in the operating room. He saw our technique through two portals, and I remember that he asked a lot of questions. On his second visit he did his training in two portals; he was already practicing minimally invasive surgery through three portals, and so the difference, the change of the practice wasn't so radical for him, because he was already an experienced and skilled surgeon in the matter."

However, Diego describes it as a sea change, a shooting star that had crossed his path of vision ("The paper where the resident from Duke diagrammed the technique" —he still has the paper— "marked a before and after in my life"). "Yes, I understand how he sees it, but personally I think that what defines him is that he wasn't satisfied with the traditional technique, the open thoracotomy, or so to say, the status quo of surgery. Instead, he looked for something better that he knew —or at least had the intuition— existed. The same thing happened to me. When I finished my training, the only thing being done was open surgery. There was no video-assisted lobectomy, but I had the same intuition: everything can be improved, you just need to figure it and apply it. And that is what I did, and I learned it for myself. It all consisted of making small, rather than large, incisions, and looking through a camera instead of directly, and gradually improving the technique. We had to discover from which angles it was best practiced, how to adapt the instrument, etcetera. The next thing I knew, we could do the operation through two ports."

Diego learned the technique from him, and after hundreds of operations through two ports (the last 40 without using the second incision), he reached the conclusion that just one was enough. He then reported to the master. And what did the master D'Amico think then? "It seemed like a logical evolution, although for me, it is still simpler to operate through two holes. I've designed a technique that is halfway between both: it's called Modify Uniportal, which consists of making two incisions, but in the same intercostal space, so that, in my opinion, it's easier for your assistant to keep the camera in the exact and correct place." Doctor D'Amico emphasizes what in his opinion is fundamental to this surgical revolution. "What is crucial is spreading the philosophy of minimally invasive surgery versus the open thoracotomy. In this regard, Diego's commitment to disseminating information and teaching, his international crusade with Uniportal VATS is a commendable and crucial effort. In addition, his character, his lifestyle is fundamental for this to happen: continually traveling is not comfortable at all for anybody, but it's easier to get out of your daily comfort if you're single, don't have kids and you're not leaving behind a family that needs you every day. I think Diego can meet this challenge because of his personality. Although of course, he never abandons his medical responsibilities here in A Coruña, which does add stress to his trips. He is definitely a very generous person, not just with his time. His humility is admirable, because otherwise it wouldn't be possible."

It is the fourth time that the American doctor has visited and given a course in the Galician city. This time, he has come with his daughter. This morning, they went for a run along the Rías Baixas (south estuaries) with its charming white sand beaches. His children both want to study in Spain —such is the fascination that the friendship between Diego and their father has generated in them. The friendship and the climate, landscape and character, and of course, the gastronomy of Spain, like the unforgettable meal they'd enjoy that night.

✳✳✳

However, first we need to return to the operating room, where, like people, the odor of the animal bodies has filled the room, as their fluids meet the air. Surgeons say that we humans smell even worse. Diego is teaching at the table he shares with Rasa, the promising young Lithuanian, and an African surgeon. Specifically, they are in the process of rotating the lobe. "Check out this trick. If you open the space, it will be easier for you to handle it" (as if it had a tumor, which it isn't; it's an experimental lobectomy on a healthy lung). Suddenly at another table, they hear, "Pass me the Diego!" They're referring to the dissector that an American surgical instrument firm has specifically designed for the Uniportal VATS technique, which long ago was popularized as "the Diego" in hospital centers around the world, including Spain —despite the reluctance of the medical establishment in his own country. This is what Raul Eckhout, the Dutch representative, who also globe-trots alongside Diego, tells us. A second firm, this one British, participates in today's training and presents a clamp applicator that is also specifically designed for Uniportal. On a panel at the entrance to the operating room, there is a sign that reads: González Rivas 45°, which is the angle sought to increase visibility when stapling the selected tissues. It is also inscribed on the titanium composite that the instrument is made of. According to Marc Moneaux, the Belgian man who represents the Anglo-Saxon institution —another person inseparable from Diego on his journeys around the planet— he and Diego were the first to make the initial sketch of the applicator. It was in Bulgaria after a very convoluted operation. Later, the technicians of the firm developed the prototype that they now sell for three different sizes of clips.

Diego continues, bent over the table of the African surgeon. It's his first practice with Uniportal and it's difficult for him. He doesn't lose his patience, but what on paper seems simple and safe, is frankly very complicated on these experimental tables: it requires the skill and precise movement of a Swiss watch. But when Diego himself practices what they call a subxiphoid approach, the mood completely shifts. Even from a non-expert viewpoint, Diego's skill is such that your confidence grows in medicine, and on further meditation, one's dread of the disease dissolves like tensions alleviated by the vibrations of a mantra in your sternum: everything seems so simple in his hands. The trainees have finished their first operation (later they'll practice a second on the lower lobes), and they crowd around him, stunned. In barely 10 minutes, Diego has liberated one of the sides of the lobe, and where he is dissecting and there is a danger of bleeding, he is inserting clamps: tiny staples that are later absorbed by the tissue.

At the adjacent table, the professor Alan Sihoe, Chief of Thoracic Surgery at the University of Hong Kong Shenzhen Hospital, has taken the baton from Diego, and is teaching four young trainees. Shortly thereafter, again in the waiting room of the operating room, he will tell the unambiguous truth of who Diego is in Shanghai. "Diego is really popular. He's like a rock star, and not just in Shanghai, but throughout China."

***

His Chinese name is Xiao Gang, which means "Little González" (Xiao means little, and Gang is an abbreviation for Ganzalisé, which is how his last name is pronounced in the Cantonese language). Just as Asian names have their Western equivalents, normally in English, to facilitate communication, Diego has been rechristened in his adopted continent, like his Shanghaian brother, Yang-Yang, who is known in the western hemisphere as Tim Young.

"He's a rock star!" Alan Sihoe explains. "The economic boom in China has created some really high expectations of medicine. After so many years of economic decline due to the Cultural Revolution and the unrelenting communist system, the Chinese now have money and want to have the best surgery on the planet. Several years ago, they started to implement the conventional video-assisted technique in thoracic surgery, but they were determined to have the best of the best, which today is Uniportal VATS. This is how this technique became so in demand and so celebrated. Diego was in the exact right place at the exact right time." He would know –he was the professor from Hong Kong who got the Galician surgeon started at Shanghai Pulmonary Hospital, where he gives an international training program every two months. They would give whatever it takes to have him permanently at the head of the thoracic surgery unit at their hospital, which is the biggest pulmonary medical center in the world. "Yes, I did introduce Diego to China." But let's find out who Professor Sihoe is, where he comes from and where he was going when he heard the first presentation by that young Spanish surgeon at one of the Asian conferences which he attended regularly. "I think it was in Bali, yes, in Bali, in late 2010." Alan Sihoe was born 43 years ago in Hong Kong, grew up in Canada, and studied Medicine at Cambridge. He cut his teeth in the medical field in the United Kingdom. In the 1990's, by the time he returned to the former British colony in Asia, he was already a skilled thoracic surgeon who practiced video-assisted surgery. At the end of that decade, he started a new professional period that would lead to him publishing numerous scientific articles and frequently participate in international symposiums. At the same time, he developed a microscopic technique to apply conventional video-assisted surgery through three portals. "Then I met Diego, such an enthusiastic person, passionate for his work, and we immediately became friends. At that time, I had already started to practice through two holes, and quickly adopted his Uniportal technique. I remember that he asked if I had any interesting contacts in China, and I did know the Head of the Thoracic Surgery Unit of the Shanghai Pulmonary, Doctor Jiang Gening, who at that time was already the head of the biggest service in the world for thoracic surgery" (Sihoe is considered one of the greatest Asian masters in the field). "The Shanghai Pulmonary Hospital, as I mentioned earlier, was very interested in reaching the highest surgical level possible, and given their difficulty with western languages, that is, with English, I was something like their bridge to the rest of the world."

Dr. Sihoe didn't have to think too long about it: one year later he had tied up all of the loose ends and was on his way. It was a Saturday morning in January 2012. They had organized a master surgery class in the Shanghai Pulmonary operating rooms taught by three instructors: Diego González, Alan Sihoe and Professor C.C. Liu, Taiwanese, father of the subxiphoid surgery. "We operated three cases of live surgery, and then the three of us went out to lunch later. We were really happy with the results. When we returned to the hospital to check on the patients, we couldn't believe it. The Pulmonary Team had operated on eight more cases by Uniportal VATS, with total success. This is characteristic of the teams in Shanghai: they have excellent basic skills, and they have so much opportunity to practice in hospitals, that they learn and perfect like nobody else in the world." And that was the basis of Diego's desire to establish contact with the Chinese health system. "It's great to come here to A Coruña, the resources are good, the place is perfect, but it's there where the volume of work allows me to teach and disseminate the technique, in order to reach a greater number of surgeons. In Shanghai, the average number of daily thoracic surgery cases is 50, which adds up to more than 10,000 major operations per year." It was the perfect place to establish a base to teach the technique from, to receive surgeons from all over the world, where they can operate at a crazy pace, but in the best technical conditions. Sihoe is now an invited professor of the Shanghai Pulmonary Hospital, where one week per month, he gives a training, and also attends Diego's bimonthly training without fail. Along with the childlike Tim, Doctor Xung or Young, they form a triumvirate —ADT (Alan-Diego-Tim)— the name of the group chat they have established to stay up-to-date on each other's progress and wanderings around the world.

Alan continues to reflect on how this dynamic form of teaching and learning Uniportal VATS is something that Diego González has imported to China. The country is tremendously grateful to the Spanish surgeon and receives him with open arms, because he brings the best international surgeons to practice not only to Shanghai, but to all corners of China, where he travels as well. The international surgeons benefit from the facilities that the Chinese health system provides them to learn from. "Today, if you want to learn, you have to go to China," and he gives an example of the surgeon, who has now become a professor, Mr. Luis Hernández, of Mexico City. He has been at Shanghai

Pulmonary Hospital for nine months, and there will come a day, in the not too distant future, when he'll become the greatest professor in Latin America, at his young age (39 years). "I greatly admire Diego," he continues, "but among all of his excellent qualities, there is one I hold above the others: he's never satisfied with what he knows. Instead, he's always looking to learn more and improve. That's how all of this started, that's how he took his first steps. Now he's a celebrity for having invented the single port lobectomy, yet he's still not satisfied. He keeps learning, he is a master in the subxiphoid approach, for example, and tubeless surgery. He's never afraid; what he wants is to never stop learning." Besides, it's not just a technique. "No, of course not. Uniportal VATS is a technique, and it is very good, yes, and it is important that it progresses from three ports to one single port, yes, but the key to this revolution is without a doubt the revitalization of surgery. The important thing is transmitting a message to the surgeons: don't be content with what you already know. Don't just operate and go home calmly at five in the afternoon. No, there will always be something else you can do for the patient, because the good of the patient is our only reason for existing. Diego is a great example of this philosophy behind Uniportal. It's not difficult to teach the technique, it's not difficult to learn it either, but there is a crucial condition, and that is that the surgeon leaves their comfort zone and instead of going home at five p.m. to put their slippers on, they need to keep learning." Alan Sihoe looks inside the operating room, where a mélange of surgical caps is bobbing up and down over eight tables during the second lobectomies of the day. "What is it those people are doing?" he asks out loud. "Those people are here because they believe in the good of the patient. They earn good salaries, their lives are comfortable and satisfactory, but they are convinced that they can always take another step for the good of the patients, and that is what matters. That's why they take the trouble, they leave their comfort zones and come to learn."

Both Dr. Sihoe and Professor Amico's own experiences are an exemplar of this. "Look. Since a young age, I have appeared in medical publications about conventional video-assisted surgery, but I didn't stop there; I could have lived a life full of comfort, but that's not what really satisfies me. Let's look at Professor D'Amico. He invented the video-assisted technique through two ports and put Duke on the international map for surgery, but he continued evolving, and shortly thereafter, he modified his own technique (Modify Uniportal). All of us that are in the operating room, some younger, some older, it makes no difference, we share this philosophy of advancing, and this is the spirit that matters most. Why are we here? Because we want to do things better." They do them and teach them. "90% of surgeons do their work in the operating room, and that satisfies them sufficiently. There is another 10% that are more interested in research, and we want to transmit everything that we've learned throughout our career, and that's why we write in scientific journals about our discoveries. Beyond that, there is 2% within that 10%, which includes Diego, who are not content with publishing but dedicate their efforts to spreading the message and making sure it reaches everyone who wants to listen and learn. Over the generations, there have been surgeons with these exceptional characteristics. My mentor in Hong Kong, Doctor Anthony P.C. Yim (one of the few Asian members of the elite AATS which Diego González has just accessed), was a pioneer of video-assisted surgery in the early 1990's and worked hard to propagate it throughout Asia. Each generation has its stars, and the one of our generation is without a doubt Diego. He's our global star, and it's very rejuvenating that something like this is happening."

It goes beyond the generosity of disseminating your own findings. "Yes, of course, it's a very generous choice. Many others would feel threatened to share their discoveries, as if by doing them someone were going to steal their business. Obviously, that's a mistake, because sharing your abilities can never be prejudicial, and even less so in the case of Diego. His medical practice is very prosperous and offers him a good quality of life." But there is something else, a higher ethical calling: the feeling of responsibility. "We (he's referring to Diego, D'Amico and himself) feel responsible for disseminating our developments, for spreading the knowledge we've acquired during our career. It's something like thinking: look, in my surgery room, I can save 10 lives, but if I come here and I teach how to do this to another 10 surgeons, maybe we'll be saving 100. And this would be the summary of the vitality that moves Diego, the passion that drives him, his life philosophy."

At this point in the conversation, as he lifts his gaze above the glass that separates the waiting room from the operating rooms, where the activity continues frenetically, Professor Alan Sihoe reflects. "Look at him. Always so happy and excited. It's something that amazes me about him. It's incredible but he has this natural friendliness which has confused more than a few people, who without knowing him well consider him superficial, and think he's not serious. I can assure you that he's one of the most serious surgeons I've met in my entire life and is without a doubt the most dedicated to medicine. When he gets something in his head, he doesn't stop until he achieves it. I'll give you an example. Look at his physical appearance. He's so athletic, so thin and strong. When I met him up close, four years ago, Diego wasn't like that. It's not like he was fat, but a little thicker. It was when he had started traveling non-stop, the lack of routine with meals and the little time he had exercise started to take its toll. So, he told himself, 'I'm going on a diet to improve my health.' I can assure you that the next time we met, I couldn't believe it, but I was like, 'Diego, you're so skinny!' Yeah, since then, he's been taking extremely good care of his diet, as hard as that is when you eat out every day, but he's very strict and his food is very healthy. When Tim and I go to eat dinner with him (the triumvirate, also known as the Three Musketeers), well, we love to eat (both are, let's say, on a good day, stocky, maybe a bit overweight), but he knows how to say what isn't good for him, and never eats to excess. This is what he also applies to surgery. When he wants to improve some aspect, as insignificant as the detail may appear, and no matter how long the day of surgery was, he comes to these experimental operating rooms with his team, saying, 'alright, let's go practice!' and they don't stop until they get what they look for, which is always to perfect. And the team follows him, because he has been able to bring together a group of absolutely exceptional people, stupendous, who without a doubt deserve the success they are having.

"When he's in Shanghai, he also doesn't stop perfecting. He doesn't skip even the most minor opportunity to improve, to introduce new features, and he never gets tired. We're talking about work days in China that start at 8 in the morning, never finish before 8 at night, and may even stretch beyond midnight. Everyone is half-dead, and he's always engaged and happy."

Just then, Luis Hernández leaves the operating room. Alan calls him to join the conversation and describe how they work there, where he's been for nine intense months. The surgeon from Mexico City, who has resettled in China, speaks. "Normally, we don't finish before midnight, because at Shanghai Pulmonary Hospital, there are no cancellations. You work until your list of scheduled cases ends. The longest day I remember is when we finished at 4:30 in the morning, and at 6:00 a.m., we were leaving for Taiwan, to continue operating. Diego was so happy. He was always the one who could endure the most, the most enthusiastic. He has limitless energy." You stay behind, or you follow him, and Luis follows him. Luis is also single, like Diego, and also lives for surgery. There's a bet going around the circles of surgeons about which one will tire first. Alan tells me between laughs, "Wherever Diego goes, all doctors and nurses want to have their picture taken with them. 'You haven't seen them?'" You can see it on his Facebook page, a page that doesn't accept more followers, because it's at full capacity.

Alan, on the other hand, is married to an operating room nurse. They met in the operating room —as if it could be any other way. He has a 9-year-old son that he misses a lot. He prefers not to think about it —this May, he's only been at home for five days. "The only thing I don't want is for him to also end up being a doctor," but it's very likely.

The colleague from Hong Kong does not stop mentioning another of the aspects that characterizes his friend: "What do you think he does between one operation and another? You might think he'd relax, rest, I don't know.

But no, he writes. He's an indefatigable spreader of knowledge. He leaves the operating room and he writes up the case, he edits the video of the operation, and posts it on his YouTube page. His publications are fantastic and have greatly contributed to thoracic surgery. In China, they're compiling a collection that is a faithful reflection of his spirit. He communicates, and the whole world follows his steps, day in, day out, development bit by bit. He's just a rock star!"

A rock star dressed in green scrubs, who "changed the form of operating in the most important hospital in the world!" Doctor Sihoe is talking about Shanghai Pulmonary. In light of his words, let's remember the old English phrase declaring that luck occurs when preparation and ability meet at an auspicious time: "That's what we call luck! When preparation meets opportunity."

***

The same saying could be applied to what happened that April to Zoya Lobanova, 81 years of age, American of Russian origin. She is a resident of Los Angeles, the city of Doctor Robert McKenna, who dared to perform the first video-assisted lung surgery in 1992 at Cedars Sinai Medical Center, and whom Diego met in his first exposure to non-invasive surgery. The quintessential master, McKenna's statistics of successful operations are still awe-inspiring (only less than 0.8% of some 3,000 lobectomies did not have the expected result). However, because of her advanced age, and some technical complications associated with her tumor, Zoya was not strong enough to be able to withstand a thoracic operation with general anesthesia and three incisions. According to the case records, her survival in the operating room was not at all certain.

Not only was Zoya in the city of Los Angles, but she was a patient of master McKenna at Sinai Medical Hospital. "We tried to seek out a second opinion, despite being aware that we were in the best hands, in the best department in California," writes Zoya from Los Angeles. "We started to research, and that's how, with the help of my daughter Lilia, we found a series of medical articles written by doctors Diego González Rivas and César Bonome. They explained the tubeless Uniportal VATS technique without assisted breathing: minimal invasion, quick recovery, painless, two days of hospitalization... It seemed like science fiction, but instead of speculating, we wrote an email to Doctor González. To our wonderful surprise, we almost immediately received a fantastic, intimate response. After studying the tests we had sent him, he told us that it would be best for us to go to A Coruña. Of course, we had never heard of the place, which seemed to be in a corner of northern Spain (where the Romans founded Finisterrae, the end of the world). It was going to be quite an adventure, so we talked it over with the Doctor McKenna."

"The master," this is Diego speaking now, "was absolutely gracious. He told them they would be in good hands, and that I was his disciple. He convinced them to do the 5,500-mile trip from California to Spain. I just needed to find time for them in the operating room in A Coruña." In April, a window opened up between his trip to four cities in Israel and the course in Croatia. He had barely two or three days in Galicia, but even still, the scarce time would be sufficient to operate.

"The communication that followed the first email," continues Zoya from Los Angeles "was even more surprising, because of the transparency, his humility, the amount of information that he provided us without us even presuming to ask. And the most incredible part, was that in addition to his expert talent, he even found us accommodation and organized the logistics of our trip! He did all that as he was traveling from one end of the planet to another, and he did so with such friendliness and sense of humor that my daughter and I prepared the trip as if we were going on vacation. I mean, I can say that because I've forgotten the worst part already (a cancer that left her with barely a few more months to live). All of a sudden, we had landed in a beautiful city, a hospital with incredible views over the beach and estuary, and when they discharged me, we both stayed in a hotel five minutes from Diego and his magnificent team. Three days later he had to leave again." Not only did they receive a curative surgery, but the positive energy from the exceptional medical team was infectious: Zoya and her daughter Lillian were filled with the desire to embrace life. At this point in the story, this fact has become a constant that is repeated throughout each one of the patients that pass through his hands.

It's commonplace with Diego: he not only operates on them, but he hosts them if necessary, as he did with the Russian Eugène Abdullin, the young teacher with a potentially deadly congenital tumor on his lung to whom he restored his strength. The doctor is a great guide in his city: he arranges the best lodgings, located specifically to facilitate the two or three post-operative visits; a pleasant accommodation that has gradually become Diego's international base of operations: patients, conference-goers, students in his courses, etcetera, all stay at Hotel Ática.

**

To continue with the case of Zoya —once again, the pain had been their *leitmotif*. Her daughter Lilian, American by origin of Russian ancestry, and an executive at Fox (the filmmaking giant) remembers. "My mother was very afraid of pain and anesthesia in general. Deep inside, I think she was afraid of a premature farewell, without being able to say goodbye. The operation in A Coruña, with a doctor who was so sincere, frank and approachable, gave her the assurances that the other doctors didn't. We never could have imagined that 48 hours after the totally successful operation, with her discharge papers in her pocket, and with Diego reachable at any time on Facetime, my mom and I would decide to go for a walk along the coastal path around the town. As we walked, we were overcome with happiness: it was an incredible experience, one of those unrepeatable moments in life that took place over a 9-mile walk. That was the post-operative recovery, a 9-mile walk along the coast of the Atlantic Ocean. Everything seemed like science fiction, but it was real, it was happening."

They stayed another two weeks in the city, enjoying the randomness of life, accumulating so much positive energy that, upon returning to Los Angeles, Zoya wrote a letter of gratitude that was published in the local newspaper, *La Voz de Galicia*. It was an ode to a small city in a northwestern corner of Europe, the Finisterrae of the Roman Empire, the site of their impenetrable Tower of Hercules.

The elder Lobanova wrote in the paper about the "added bonus of that land, its landscapes, such friendly people, and delicious gastronomy. It is a 10. From the bottom of my heart, I want to thank Doctor González Rivas and his magnanimous team for their professionalism, care and dedication in the pre-operation consultations, during the operation and the recovery in the San Rafael Hospital." In that remote point of the European geography, Zoya Lobanova was resurrected, and found a life again.

CHAPTER 17:
A Non-diagnosis

When the case is non-operable, I tell them to trust in the rapid advances in medicine: I'm convinced that cancer will be eradicated as a fatal disease and is on its way to becoming a chronic ailment.

Tonight, on the corner opposite the Hotel Ática, in the restaurant Comarea, Diego is to meet with the participants of the international course he is giving in A Coruña: a troupe of masters, trainees and part of his team from Coruña University Hospital. This impersonal housing complex on the outskirts of the city, is like his second home —with its slight pretension of being a financial district (Amancio Ortega, owner of Zara group, discreetly has breakfast here every day at a private club). Here Diego moves like a fish in water, or like he himself when he gets the chance to swim in the water, his favorite element.

The Taiwanese man Ching Feng Wu and the Lithuanian woman Rasa are waiting punctually at the door to the restaurant, two of his fervent disciples of the course. Wu was sent here by his superiors to do a one-year residency at A Coruña Hospital. He discovered the technique in one of the courses Diego gave in Shanghai three years prior. He's capable of performing surgery by himself, but they preferred him to be the one to perfect Diego's technique, to be able to teach it in Taiwan. He is explaining to Rasa how language is not only useful for teaching purposes, but also an essential facet of praxis -communication with the patient. "Here, everybody speaks in Spanish or Galician, and very few patients and family members understand me when I express myself in English, and this interaction with the patients is a vital part of our job." Rasa would like to be able to come like her Taiwanese colleague for an entire year to learn UniVATS. Diego visited them for the first-time last October in Vilnus, and since then, the thoracic team of the first medical center of the Lithuanian capital has been set-up with the necessary instruments, but they still don't dare to implement the practice. "I've barely participated in two lobectomies, I still cannot do it by myself," says Rasa, 27 years old, with cobalt blue eyes that transmit her sincerity.

Little by little, a large group congregates and walks in a procession from the hotel to the door of the restaurant, where the most sumptuous seafood from these coasts are served: shrimp, king crab filled with roe, female mussels, grilled razor shell clams... Most have never seen these crustaceans, mollusks and bivalves up close, but nobody hesitates to dive in. As the sublime delicacies melt in their mouths, they burst into praise. It's like eating the wild sea, bit by bit.

Tim Young, the young Chinese brother, is seated at the table of honor, in his role as master —the youngest, but a master nonetheless. He is shy, especially with women. Diego is always watching over him, like he would for a younger brother to protect him. They banter back and forth with Professor Sihoe, around the circular and resplendent table —la grande bouffe. In an adjacent room, a group of Polish doctors are sharing a dinner, the team of Joana Lipinska, an extraordinarily beautiful woman with delicate features between Anglo-saxon and Slavic, with several Belarussian surgeons and Doctor Juan Carlos Collado from Havana, who tells us that Diego is considered like a prime minister in his country: "He's the guest of honor. Because, what does a president or prime minister bring? Normally, nothing. And him? He brought a medical revolution to Cuba. He's demonstrated that it's not necessary to inflict so much pain on the patient. He has given us an example, and despite the initial reluctance, thanks to Diego and the legion of young surgeons that are following in his footsteps (you don't need to look any farther than these tables), today almost 50% of the thorascoscopic lobectomies in the world are done through Uniportal VATS," he says whenever he has the chance.

***

The next morning after the sumptuous supper, the training course centers on performing two surgeries broadcast live from the operating rooms of A Coruña Hospital to the assembly hall on the ground floor of the building, in real time, following minute-by-minute the life hanging in the balance on the operating table. The first is an upper left lobectomy, which is carried out successfully and without any mishap. Alan Sihoe is in the hall, leading the conversation with Diego; through questions and answers they turn the case into a teachable example of the technique. The questions are cleverly formulated by the Doctor from Hong Kong: he and Diego lead the participants from one question to another.

The second case is an obese patient around 80 years-old. A pulmonary nodule has been detected whose origin is unclear, but has a very high uptake (uptake, remember, is what measures the cancerous activity of the tissues). For reasons they don't go into, the tumor wasn't possible to diagnose; however, he was admitted for surgery, because it is likely malignant. The thoracic surgery team and oncologists decide to operate as soon as possible. They will use endotracheal intubation this time, because the patient was a smoker up until two years ago, when he was diagnosed with emphysema, and therefore, the lungs themselves are damaged and his capacity to breathe is reduced.

The next thing you know, they're inside and working on the nodule: a bulbous and dark mass. "It's surely malignant," can be heard over the speakers in the conference room. They cut the adhesions, and insert it into a condom-like sack, remove it and immediately send it to the pathology department for analysis. Until the result comes, they continue exploring, and find a series of stains, which they remove to analyze. All of them are a dark and concerning color. "I don't like the way this looks," Diego says in the room, and asks, "What do we do if the first nodule is definitely positive?" The opinion is divided, most say that a lobectomy should be done. A second malignancy appears, which is removed, and then a third lymph node station that is stuck to the trachea. These make him fear the worst: there are lymph nodes, the cancer has metastasized. "Honestly," Diego asks again, "what do we do if the first and second are positive?" Doctor Sihoe opts to do the lobectomy no matter what, as other surgeons begin to ask how these other tumors haven't been detected in radiological tests. A tomblike silence overtakes the room, you can only hear the noise of the instruments dissecting, and the beep-beep that keeps the patient on assisted breathing. Meanwhile, Diego's scalpel has reached an area that is rarely accessed, the deep contralateral subcarinal space, and again there is metastasis. The first result has arrived: malignant. Alan speaks from the room: "Diego, if you're concerned, before continuing to remove, wait for the second biopsy." It has just arrived —also positive. It's then that Alan's opinion shifts. "I don't understand the benefit of continuing to remove stations." "Yes," Diego responds, "I'll finish this one... No, actually it isn't helping his case much anymore. We shouldn't do the lobectomy." It would be worse for the patient given the chemotherapy treatment that he will have to undergo. It's one of those cases that they call "undiagnosed," and that unfortunately are more frequent than expected. These are cases in which the PET scan and other diagnostic tests do not give a conclusive result, thus hiding the real situation. Specifically, in this patient, they had only detected uptake on a pulmonary nodule, which appeared to be the only one, without any assumed lymphatic involvement. Therefore, they thought they could perform surgery. However, in the surgery room, it was discovered that in addition to having a pulmonary tumor, there was a proliferation of lymph nodes suspected of being malignant that after being biopsied, ended up all being cancerous. "No," Diego would explain, "it's not an erroneous diagnosis, but an undiagnosed case, or an underdiagnosed case. Unfortunately, it's not uncommon for certain tumors to not show up, they are hidden in even the most advanced tests."

Diego is likely thinking about how to break the bad news to the family members, something that luckily, he's not very accustomed to doing. Normally, he operates when he is sure, because of the enormous risk entailed in each one of the complicated cases that he operates. And how can one not think about it. The patient is a human being, whom he had taken the time to get to know even though he had only been in the city for three days. He had arrived to give a course, and this is its twisted finale. The patient outside the operating room is not just a case, something to check off a list, or a number for Doctor González. Diego would tell the patient and his family members, like he does in the non-operable cases that he sees, that surgery is not the best option in his situation. "I advise them to continue with the treatment, medicine advances very fast these days. In fact, I'm convinced that cancer will be eradicated as a fatal disease, and that it's on its way to becoming a chronic ailment. I tell them to have faith. Even though it's not an operable case; I could remove segments or lobes, but that isn't right. They need to maintain hope because oncology gives surprises every day." The auditorium empties.

CHAPTER 18:
This Is How It All Began

Those who succeed have no room for laziness. It's better to regret something you did, than something you didn't do because you weren't sure. You learn from your mistakes.

There is a photograph in Doctor González Rivas' family album that defines him like no other moment does. The photo illustrates part of his Ted Talk when he refers to one of the three cornerstones of his life: a restless kid who from a very young age shows his curiosity for technology.

He has just arrived in A Coruña, where he will work for 13 days (on arrival, he is immediately on-call, and works one mandatory shift after another), gratefully soaking in the warmth from his dear family. Between work and family, Diego of course relishes the waves and friendships at the beach, where *Dieguini* is of course at the center of it all. There is no surfer or lifeguard who doesn't know him and they all head over to give him a high-five. His stay at home is only interrupted by a lightning-fast trip to Beijing to confer and sign contracts, like we said earlier, for the founding statutes of the Asiatic Society of Thoracic Surgery. He leaves on a Friday and returns on Monday, and once back, he continues to operate, take appointments, do his rounds, surf, enjoy his lovely and much-needed family in his hometown.

Diego is driving his car (his surfboard always inside, like part of the furniture), on his way to the family's summer home in the municipality of Bergondo. It's next to the sea and is surrounded by forests and forest trails like Pan's Labyrinth minus Pan. A gynecologist can be heard on the car speakers, connected to the cell phone, asking if he can see one of his most valued patients, sick from cancer, who may have a minuscule node on his lung. Diego receives many calls like this throughout the day. He recommends that the patient come to his office before he travels again in less than one week. This time his adventures are taking him far away.

In Bergondo, the land of Sanín, parish of Lubre, an image suddenly resurfaces of Diego as a child, 3 years old, flared blue jeans, sitting with his little legs that barely reach the side of the yellow, seventies-style easy chair; in one hand, a red bakelite telephone, in the other, a racing motorcycle. The photo shows up in the face of a 63-year-old woman, with a radiant, youthful look, who appears at the porch of the country house where she summers with the entire family (minus Diego, who comes and goes from the world, and from his terraced house, perfect for a single and independent man). She is of the same mold as Diego: her smile, her expression is of a smart woman who has learned from life. Pilar Rivas is an institution in the Maternal and Children's Hospital of A Coruña. She had a 43-year career as a nurse, sometimes a supervisor, in the postpartum department. She wears thick glasses with a dramatic red frame. The similarity between Diego and his mother is immediately apparent.

His family is waiting for him to eat lunch —three servings of mussels, homemade empanada made with home-canned tuna, rice with cuttlefish caught that morning in the Sada estuary by Uncle Manolo and a pear compote from their garden with cinnamon. Everything goes down like holy water, including the albariño white wine from the slopes of south Galicia, the local aromatic herb liquor, while the fathers, uncles, aunts, sister and brother-in-law, nephews and a few close friends of the family gather and tell stories about the childhood and youth of that curious kid whom they define as "uncontainable. No one could control him, us included, of course," his aunts say. His patient father, with his solid, distinguished features, sits on the side-lines of the female-dominated household, run by his wife, his two sisters and "Godmother" —great aunt and adoptive mother of Pilar (their parents have been gone since their emigration to Venezuela; she only saw their father three times in her live, and the mother once more, when she passed away and she went to collect and give away things because Chavez and his cronies didn't allow a cent to leave that country).

"He wanted to be an actor and singer, but not a professional singer, he wanted to sing songs like construction workers and he wanted to be a school bus driver. Later when the TV show 'One, Two, Three...' started, he tried to be gallant to attract its star —La Bombi," remembers his aunt and godmother María José.

"And when did he first get his calling?"

"When he was 7 years-old, he had two main interests, he wanted to make people laugh and heal people," says his aunt Laura, the youngest on his father's side. "He would lock himself in my room at my parents' house, because he slept with me when we were in the Penamoa house, and he would take a cassette player from that era, and a microphone, and he'd record tapes of jokes and speeches and end by saying, 'I hope you've enjoyed yourselves, and that no family member dies'."

When Diego's mother was making her rounds, which were constant in the postpartum departments, the aunts took care of the child, so it was up to them to try to tame his genius and stubbornness. For example, one time, when he was a kid, they had to rush to remove him from the waves in Riazor. He was purple and shivering from the cold, and people were emptying the beach in search of shelter because a storm was approaching, but Diego shouted that he wanted to stay in the rumbling sea (which swallows up more than a few every year). People looked at them as if to say, what are those crazy women doing with that child? Or on Wednesdays when Aunt Laura used to take him to the Avenue Cinema, close to the pharmacy where she still works. The child arrived at the theater and wanted to sit alone in the first row. Then in the middle of the movie, he turned to yell to his aunt far behind him to say, "Auntie, the movie is pretty cool, huh?" Everyone in the room glared at him. Such embarrassing situations they had to go through! "You see! The kid was already showing signs of what was to come," says Laura.

Embarrassing moments included the day when he ridiculed a man with dwarfism: "Look at you. Look at what happened because you didn't eat!" Or the time he tugged on a blind man's jacket and asked, "Can you see me? Can you see me? Why can't you see me?" His aunts reprimanded him, and the child explained, "Aunties, I want to behave well, but I don't know what happens: I just can't." Since his ability to use reason, he has had a passion for discovery, an insatiable curiosity. He explains it by referring to the Golden Circle by Simon Sinek. "Everything starts by asking the 'why' behind things."

During one of his Uniportal VATS courses in A Coruña, he was approached by one of his students, a Dutch surgeon, who had been watching him carefully. He told him why he was motivated to attend the course and get to know him: "I always look for the why in things, and I needed to know why something as unbelievable as this surgical technique has caused such an impact on the worldwide community and has also become a philosophy or form of behavior for surgeons. I really wanted to discover the *why*." He referred Diego to Simon Sinek's Ted Talk (the second-most watched in TED's history), about a 'golden circle,' which has become an oracle amongst leaders, which explains why some people get what others in identical or even better circumstances do not. Why do some reach their goals, and others don't. The British author, Simon Sinek, shows why by using a wide range of examples, such as Apple, the Wright brothers and Martin Luther King Jr.

"Why Doctor King Jr.? Why him and not some other African American? Why did the Wright brothers make the first airplane a reality, and then later flying would change the path of civilization? Of all the people working on the dream then, they were the least prepared. Why does Apple triumph –it's just another among hundreds of companies that manufacture technology products? The answer: because they asked the *why* in things; because they don't sell a thing, but a dream, a belief, a purpose. In his talk, Sinek draws three concentric circles. In the nucleus, there is *why*, next there is *how*, and in the outer ring is *what*. "All companies or professionals know *what* it is they do, and some are aware of *how* they do it, but very few are aware of *why* they do it. Only those who know and believe in their purpose inspire and attract others," that is, they lead. It's a circle that, he explains, is reproduced in the cerebral cortex, where the *why* corresponds to the decision and capacity to verbalize and communicate. "People do not buy what you do, they buy why you do it," the speaker repeats time and time again throughout the 15-minute talk. "And this is a biological question. When a leader, a professional or company ask the *why* of what they're doing, they are confirming what they believe."

Diego firmly believed in the possibility of improving the quality of life of patients, reducing their suffering, extending their life expectancies, and his Uniportal VATS technique simply confirms what he believes. And therefore, as his Dutch colleague pointed out, he has developed his capacity to form teams and preach the technique throughout the world, with unprecedented acceptance, following: *Keep calm and think Uniportal!*

Like a coda after the verse of Sinek's reflections, Diego adds, "It is better to regret something you've done than something you didn't do because you were unsure: you learn from your mistakes." What is Diego's *why*? To avoid suffering.

***

But we were back at the family lunch, at the Sanín country house, amongst forests and the salty breeze that rises from the estuary to the neighboring mountains, infusing the air and crops. For fun, the family recounts anecdotes of the child who "was already showing signs of what was to come," and today is one of the world's leading surgeons —a healer admired by thousands of patients. In 2015, he himself did 800 major surgeries. This year, the figure will surely be much higher, and it is already exponentially higher than his colleagues, perhaps thanks to his circle or philosophy created around Uniportal VATS. The son of an upstanding, observant father, and a vivacious but strict mother, they couldn't contain Diego by themselves, so they drew support from the family. However, neither they, nor anybody could keep up with Diego. Not even Diego could suppress his own curiosity, his sense of adventure, and his single-mindedness whilst being simultaneously flattering, charming, caring, cheerful, *argalleiro*, and beloved. José González (67 years) remembers when Mr. Muiños, Director of the Obradoiro School, showed up at the Seat car dealership that he directed until his retirement two years ago. "Look. Your son distributed pornography all over school." What? That was too much. It crossed any allowable line for a 9-year-old kid, a fifth-grade student. What are you telling me?!! Yes, his parents had just moved to what today is their home, in the neighborhood of Elviña in A Coruña, and to transport their glasses they had wrapped them in old copies of the magazine *Interviú*, with its pages alternating between investigative and political journalism and topless and nude starlets. That didn't go unnoticed by Diego, who of course retrieved the crumpled papers, flattened them out the best he could, and the next day took the contraband to school, which he distributed among his peers.

Diego's aunts take over the storytelling to relate the anecdote of the telephone booth. They're not talking about the film with Antonio Mercero and López Vázquez (*La*

Cabina), but a telephone booth in Plaza de Vigo, which had a split cable sticking out from the roof. What's that? Do I need to go up and see that strange thing? Perhaps he was envisioning a device from Star Trek, but no matter, Diego climbed up to the roof and grabbed the cable out of curiosity, which triggered an electric shock that almost struck him down. His shout alarmed his grandmother, who was taking care of him that afternoon. She did the best she could, with some help, to get the kid down from the roof: his hand was blackened, as were his eyes, filled with fear. Or there was that time that the boy, just 8 years-old, asked his Aunt Laura if she was thinking of staying single? "Why are you asking?" the aunt replied; to which he said, "Because I'm thinking of being single." "I considered her to be a very happy woman. In fact, they say that singlehood is humankind's happiest state," Diego observes about his Aunt Laura, both of whom remain unmarried to this day. "I am sure he saw that I came and went as I pleased, and I didn't have obligations like his mother, and we were both the same age. My life seemed more interesting to him." Or when he came close to burning the house down with the chemistry-game Quimicefa, because he decided not to limit himself to playing only with the compounds that came with the game as per the recommended instructions. Instead, he took it to the extreme and introduced some new elements —always experimenting and exploring. One day he wondered what would happen if he boiled the moderately explosive mixes together and put the lid on. The pot lodged in the ceiling in the hallway, luckily just missing the child's eyes when it exploded, thanks to the guardian angel that seems to be on his shoulder since he was born. At the Jardilín Nursery School close to the hospital, where his mother left him in the mornings when she didn't have the night shift (if she couldn't take him, one of the other women in the family did), he had already had the brilliant idea of trading his glasses for candies or some markers — how clever! He was an average student, but he never failed a class, nor did they force him to study. He knew how to succeed (he scored above average on his intelligence test). Instead of studying a lot, he preferred to dedicate his time to being a defense attorney and popular leader at school.

"He was always capable of achieving his goals," his father tells me now. "Stubborn to the death." "Those who succeed can't be lazy," his son reminds him. For example, when he took his mother to the department store because he wanted to show her "something." They enter, and Diego tries on a down jacket. With a wink, the store clerk tells his mother that he's been coming to the store every day for the last two weeks to try on the jacket, and she had to buy it for him. Or there was how he didn't want to conform and have the same bicycle as everyone else; instead he fell in love with the most expensive one in a famous store in central A Coruña. He went there to test-ride his bike every day, and he'd return home talking about how wonderful it was, until he got it. "And it cost 100,000 pesetas at the time!", his father exclaims (it was in 1984). After that came the scooters, and then his first car. "Alright," his father said to keep him quiet, "if you get a minimum of a 'B' grade point average (Diego was in his first year of medicine), I'll buy it for you," his father knew the deal was meaningless because his son was never interested in excelling academically. At the end of the year, when he went to pick up his son in Santiago de Compostela, Diego met him holding a car magazine in one hand and the reports of his grades in another —from A- up to A+. "There you go, Papá! You promised me, right?" His father said, "OK, Diego, but..." And Diego replied, "Did you promise me or not?" His mother was horrified, "You are really going to buy him a car?!" The next day, Diego shows up with a friend at the Seat car dealership that his father directed. "This brat is giving me a lesson," he told himself, already resigned. He bought him none other than a modern Ibiza GTI 2.0.

Barely two years before, Diego had begun to feel that medicine was his calling. He was not certain of what this meant until his mother explained it to him in depth, drawing on her vast experience: it's well-known that nursing is either a calling or it isn't possible. She told him about all the hardest parts of the healthcare profession, and she and his father suggested that he study economics or something similar, which would suit him better. But no, "It's who I am. My vocation is to be a doctor," he replied, and there was no further discussion. Pilar remembers how Diego called her the day that he donned his scrubs for his first rotation. At that time, she was suffering from the stress of having assumed the supervision of the entire Postpartum Department, "And you're calling me for this?" "Well, yeah," her son replied, "for me, it's a really important day —like looking into the future."

The relationships in this unique family are strong and close —strong enough to adopt Diego's mother, who barely knew her own parents due to emigration, like a sister. He travels endlessly from one end of the planet to the other and they are never sure where he is when they wake up; they get worried when they hear news of terrorist attacks, supposed 'natural' disasters or murders committed at the hands of disturbed people. Yet with one single text message

Diego calms them down. They, more than anyone else, know he has the capacity to endure: it's the survival of the fittest.

***

The day will have a perfect ending in A Coruña: from blood family to surf family. He makes a couple of calls and meets up with three friends to carpool to Valdaio. Along the way, the plan changes, it looks like the waves are swelling at La Cueva, in the town of Arteixo, and it's not worth going so far as Valdaio. That's the thing about surfing —it's an unexpected lover that draws you in you drop by drop. So they check out La Cueva, scan the sea's intentions and decide to make the most of the last two hours of sunlight: twilight promises barrels. Little by little, surfers start to arrive, 10, 20, up to 30 surfers and body boarders. When the tide goes down, they impetuously dive into the sea. For a long time, Diego has been a fixture atop the crests —the exact place where the waves form. One-by-one, the surfers, following the unwritten but well-known rules of courtesy, get up on their boards. In complete fusion with the water, they ride the crest of the wave, until it dies in the riptide. Long ago, surgery (teaching his surgical technique internationally) became Diego's first passion. And therefore, it's unusual to see him here and they all show their affection.

Yesterday, he entered the swell and it was very choppy. The waves were a bit disorganized, it was unusually hot during the day and the night threatened with rain. This is the divine Galicia, a different type of place. La Cueva is a beautiful beach which previously, only residents of the town of Arteixo accessed, just past the general headquarters of the giant Zara. Now, according to the lifeguards, there are days when you can count hundreds of beach-goers, spread out along the shore. That's what progress brings —roads, even if they are narrow and dangerous. However, at this late hour, only surf and body boards are gliding along the water.

We've arrived here in Oliver Méndez's car, one of Diego's inseparable buddies on the waves, companion on most of his adventures, including the terrible attack in Bali, when their lives were saved by a five-minute delay and 100 yards. Olito is his *nom-du-guerre* and he is a creative and sympathetic type, and also a textile entrepreneur. He is the author of one of the most beautifully written articles about Dieguini in the specialist magazines, *Surfer Rule*. "It's reassuring to have him close on the exotic surf trips. He's famous for his first-aid kits, in which you can find everything, everything you need. In the latest trip to Southern Maldives Island, his first-aid kit was so full, it took up an entire 8-seater table. He's a person who never fails. Whatever he says, he does; 100% adventurous and brave, he surfs huge waves and if there's a reef under the water, even better. He has friends everywhere. He's a great photographer, and he loves to upload videos (…), and if you still don't know him, someday you'll cross paths with him. You'll see that he's really a special guy."

It has been 40 very intense minutes of barrels in La Cueva and it has been a total "release" in Diego's own words. Forty minutes in communion with the force of the sea allows him to relax, like a demanding yoga session that leaves no space for thought. His strength and that of the sea, merge into one.

CHAPTER 19:
Epilogue in Front of the Sea

Enjoy each moment to the fullest. Rejoice because
every place is Here, and every moment is Now.
Siddhartha Gautama

He has barely three days left to tend to his patients in A
Coruña, and to continue enjoying his family and the waves
if he can. As he completes his rounds, Diego is honored to
accept an invitation from one of his most grateful patients:
Carmen López. She wants to introduce him to her large
family at her mother's house, a mansion on the cliff over-
looking the boulder-flanked sandy cove at the end of the
Ares estuary.

The view is like an impressionist painting —brushstrokes of green and blue of the sea. They savor a long
lunch, held in a climate of deep respect and immense gratitude toward the brilliant surgeon who has given life back
to Carmen —their daughter, wife and sister. Diego first
addresses one side of the table, then the other. On the one
side, the youngsters listen with total reverence to his surfer
anecdotes, on the other, the older ones follow his surgical
feats with unusual interest. It's like a theater, two conver-
sations at the same time, in sync, serene, wise. Carmen is

happily seated next to her savior. He is the first surgeon who didn't cause her pain, after having gone through so much surgical suffering in her 58 years of life, dating back to the polio infection she picked up when she was one and a half, and the little wooden box that her father had had built to protect the baby's leg, immobile for one month in the cradle.

Later, Carmen described "the feeling that anyone who has reached stage IV (the waiting room of terminal cancer) has at that moment in their life. I've felt so much that I've changed my perception of everything, I've received so much love from others... come on! It's like you're seeing your life passing by in a movie —for the first time, you can see how people feel about you. You can only reach this point with positive thinking, because with negativity, it's impossible."

"When they gave me the diagnosis," Carmen continues, "I stopped wearing black clothing, and I dressed up more than ever. I also immediately received incredible support from everyone, which was very important for me. Then I went to the office of a great psychiatrist friend, whom I trust a lot, and he gave me some valuable help, because you have to be 100% rational in these situations and leave your feelings aside. Each time they gave me radiation, at the start, and after chemo, in each session (48 including both treatments), I'd tell myself, 'this is going to get better, it has to get better.' When they told me that the treatments had ceased to be effective, I went back to thinking rationally and I thought, 'Let's go all out.' When a surgeon like Diego appears, and tells you, 'impossible is nothing, and surgery is the way forward. I'll operate on you...' you surrender. Now I know they've removed Rusca from my insides, and I'm aware that the cancerous gene could reappear, but if I'm sure of anything, it's that it can't ever get any worse. What could happen is that they detect it in me immediately, and they'd treat it. The big thing was to get it out of me."

***

We were at the lunch to thank Diego in front of the sea painted with impressionist brushstrokes. The entire great family's curiosity turns into a scene like a Greek chorus around the protagonist.

"Diego, does a surgeon's fear ever disappear in the operating room?"

"I would never call it fear, but respect. Nowadays, self-confidence takes its place. Operating has become almost automatic —I don't think that I'm opening up a person with feelings, but that I'm mechanically opening a thorax; it is easier with my technique, because I'm sure it doesn't cause pain."

"And hemorrhaging? What about that terrible visitor?"

"Bleeding is always a concern for a surgeon; even more so in video-assisted surgery because you don't have your hands to slow it down. You're outside the body, so you are concerned about bleeding that can put the patient's life at risk, because you have less control. However, I must say that despite that, I've published countless articles about this topic in international scientific journals, and I've given many conferences about controlling bleeding in video-assisted surgery, in which, as I said, you don't have the support of your hands. Also, blood obscures the camera. It's horrible when something like this happens. I remember a situation during a live surgery that I did in Israel.

However, I managed to control the bleeding in such a way that I posted the video on my YouTube channel, in order to teach the whole world how to resolve a situation of such complexity."

He also then remembers but doesn't talk about the terrible risks involved in Carmen's operation —a tumor encrusted on her vena cava, so severely radiated and ravaged with chemotherapy that it had become soft, fragile and vulnerable. These are cases that he prepares far in advance, study them, calmly analyze them, and make sure he has the necessary material to stop the hemorrhaging if it starts. In Carmen's case, an external circulation pump was prepared that thankfully in the end, didn't need to be used. "In these delicate situations, the most important thing is maintaining safety. However, like medicine, surgery is not an exact science."

***

It's Sunday. Tomorrow, Monday, he has two complicated patients waiting for him. One of them is a Jehovah's Witness, and according to his religious beliefs, he cannot accept a drop of transfused blood. San Rafael Hospital has a well-trained unit in handling bleeding situations. Jehovah's Witnesses prefer to die before receiving a transfusion. The second patient is another of those extreme cases that always ends up in his hands. Both patients come from far and both operations would be successful. In particular, the Jehovah's Witness has his tumor —nearly 6 inches long and 2 inches wide— removed without any bleeding at all.

"What is worse than death?"

"Death is devastating for the people who love you, but one doesn't suffer, because you're no longer there. Pain and disability are much worse than death. I'm not afraid of death, I'm afraid of suffering, from a degenerative disease, for example, or depression. Seeing life go by and not being able to enjoy it."

He already knew it, but saw it written for the first time on a trip to Tibet, which was captured in the documentary *7 Days, 7 Cities* by Daniel López, Mandeo Records: "Enjoy each moment of life to the fullest. Rejoice, because every place is Here, and every moment is Now." And yes, he believes it. "I'm happy now —tomorrow may never come."

WHAT IS THE
MARÍA JOSÉ JOVE FOUNDATION?

The María José Jove Foundation (FMJJ by its Spanish acronym) is an entity headquartered in A Coruña, Spain that has worked since 2003 on behalf of children and people with different capabilities.

It was created in memory of María José Jove Santos, a dedicated mother, worker and volunteer for several social and humanitarian causes, who passed away unexpectedly in 2002. Presided over by her sister, Felipa, her heritage is made up of family members and people close to Maria José Jove in life, committed to promoting actions that represent and consolidate the values inherited from her.

The main scope of action of the María José Jove Foundation is Galicia, and it is estimated that since it was established in 2003, more than 65,000 people have benefitted directly or indirectly from its activities. Its funding comes from contributions from patrons, third-party donations and revenue from the Rialta University Residency, owned by the foundation.

The FMJJ focuses its efforts on providing conciliation for balancing work and family, the inclusion of people with different abilities, improving healthcare for children, promoting a healthy life and strengthening the creative spirit of the youngest ones. To do so, it acts in four lines of work:

- **Healthcare.** The Foundation's medical department has among its priorities the prevention and research of diseases, especially the most severe ailments that affect children, in addition to improving their stay in hospitals, and the family circumstances that go along with them. In this environment, their support is notable for research in the field of Autism Spectrum Disorders (ASD), Obsessive Compulsive Disorder (OCD) and Attention Deficit Hyperactivity Disorder (ADHD), whose studies have been published in the magazine *Nature*, in addition to the new introduction of dogs into therapy in hospitals.
- **Responsible leisure and free time**. This department works to promote healthy life habits among young people and people with different capabilities. Since 2007, the MJJF has developed a pioneer project that has become a reference in Spain and provides the opportunity to practice sports to people with different capabilities from any age range. It has a winter calendar with swimming, fitness, sailing, kayaking and hiking activities, and another one for summer, which also includes beach assistance.
- **Education and training.** The FMJJ is committed to programs that promote inclusion and facilitate the balance between work and family life. Notable projects include programs for families on childhood development, helping children and teens to

manage their emotions and training teachers to be emotionally sensitive in the classroom.

- **Cultural promotion.** The Foundation develops an intense cultural activity with initiatives designed to promote through Art, the inclusion of people with different capabilities or at risk of exclusion. The axes of action are to support talented youth and to awaken a creative spirit in the youngest ones. In addition, the FMJJ is home to a distinguished and private collection of modern and contemporary art (from the 19th to the 21st Century). Owned by Manuel Jove —father of both, María José and Felipa— it has been loaned to the FMJJ temporarily to disseminate it for educational and cultural purposes.

DR. DIEGO'S CRUSADE IN PICTURES

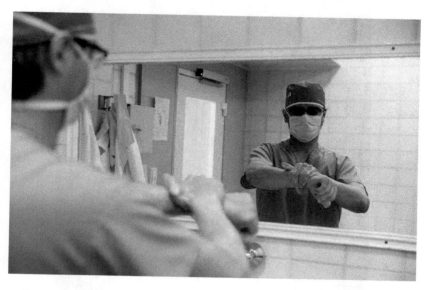

Doctor Diego González during the pre-surgery wash; pensive, focused, because awaiting him in the operating room is a complex tubeless surgery (without mechanical ventilation) that will be broadcast live to the auditorium at the Annual Cardiothoracic Surgery Conference in Saint Petersburg, June 2015. (Author's archive)

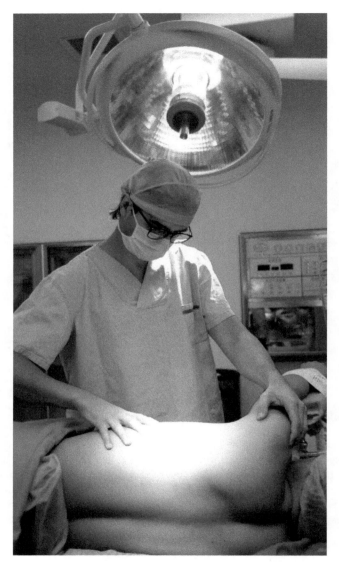

Assessing where to make an incision in a patient inside the operating room. This photograph is from one of the bi-monthly training courses at Shanghai Pulmonary Hospital. (Daniel López)

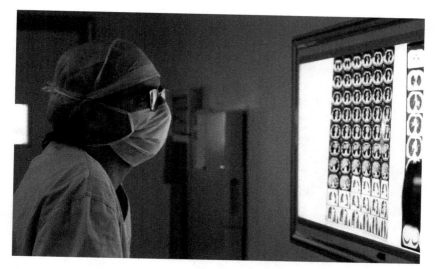

Diego studies the CT scan of a complex tumor that he is about to operate at Nanjing Chest Hospital, Jiangsu, China. (Daniel López)

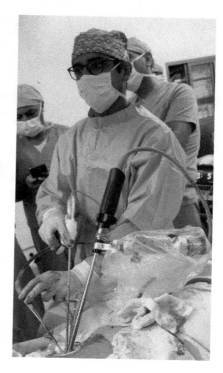

Doctor González Rivas introduces a new innovation: a robotic articulated arm that allows him to perform Uniportal VATS without the help of an assistant. It was presented during a training session at the Shanghai Pulmonary Hospital, September 2016. (Daniel López)

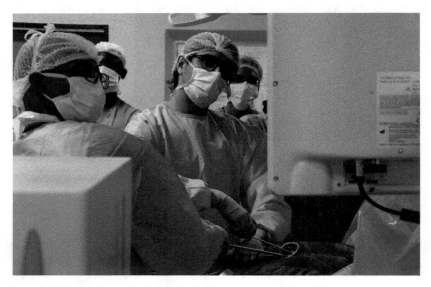

Practicing the first subxiphoid surgery at George Mukhadi Hospital in Pretoria (South Africa), August 2016. "He was a young patient with a 12 cm tumor that looked like a thymoma (neoplasia of the thymus, extremely rare). The subxiphoid approach through the Uniportal VATS technique was a worldwide innovation that we had developed at Shanghai Pulmonary Hospital. The surgeons in the master class asked if they could perform the surgery in order to learn. It was a huge challenge, without the appropriate instruments, but I tried and it turned out well. They thanked me profusely." (Author's archive)

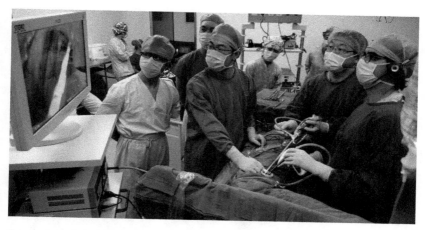

Surgery broadcast live to the Nanjing Chest Hospital auditorium in Jiangsu (China) in January 2016. Diego's images and commentaries are broadcast in real time to the participants in the Uniportal VATS course, who ask questions about the case and operation, and thus the surgery becomes educational. This time, it was an upper left lobectomy. (Daniel López)

The welcome received from the thoracic surgery team of the Changzhou No. 2 People's Hospital in Jiangsu on April 23, 2016, where a master class was held during a live surgery. (Author's archive)

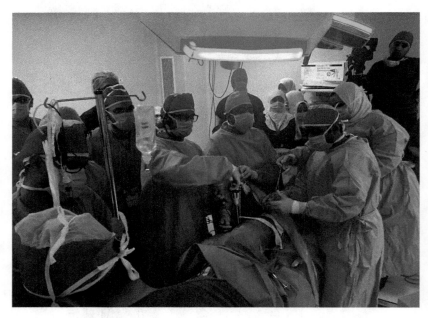

The first Uniportal VATS master class in Egypt, February 2016. Doctor González operates live on a very complex case at Assiut Heart University Hospital. "It made me sweat. It was a large central tumor on the lower and middle lobes of the right lung. I tried to preserve the upper lobe, but it was impossible and finally, I had to remove the entire lung. However, the patient recovered well." (Author's archive)

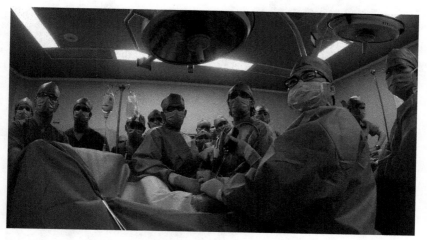

Operating room in one of the training programs that Doctor González leads in Shanghai. It is held every two months, and at each one, an average of twenty surgeons from all over the world are trained for two weeks. Shanghai Pulmonary Hospital is the largest thoracic surgery center in the world. There are twelve operating rooms in which a daily average of between forty and fifty patients are operated on each day. Diego operates on three, and sometimes up to five cases per day. (Daniel López)

Cover of *Namibia Sun*, the main newspaper of Namibia, June 2016. It was the first thoracoscopic surgery performed in the country. Doctor González removed an entire lung through Uniportal VATS. (Author's archive)

The cover of the newspaper *Oriental Daily* after the first Asian conference of Uniportal VATS in Hong Kong, 2013. "It was a total success, and the start of Uniportal's expansion into Asia. It was after this conference when Shanghai Pulmonary Hospital contacted me and invited me to give a talk and operate in their center." (Author's archive)

News bulletin in Russia. News about a live surgery from Saint Petersburg, specifically a tubeless single-port lobectomy. (Author's archive)

Gaceta Krakoska, of Zakopane (Poland). News about the first Uniportal VATS master class in this city, in June 2016. Several tubeless single-port lobectomies were performed, including one through the neck. (Author's archive)

Report in the Xiamen Newspaper (China). (Author's archive)

Interview at the door to the operating room for a Chinese news station. (Daniel López)

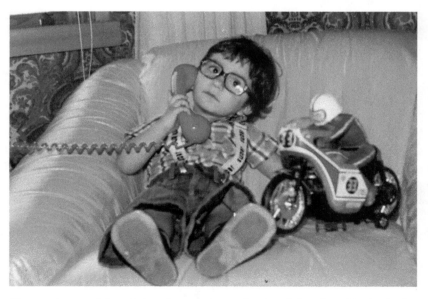

Diego at the age of three. It is perhaps the image that best defines him. That's why the surgeon included it in his Ted Talk to explain the origins of his crusade. "One must know his own past to understand the present and guide the future." (Author's archive)

Giant waves in Mentawai (Indonesia), 2005. "The day they took that picture of me, I was about to die. We spent two weeks on a boat, surfing all day, baked by the sun. It was the last day there and I remember I felt tired. But I saw one of those perfect waves coming, and the pro who caught it had fallen, leaving it open for me. I turned around and started riding it. It was enormous, with a huge tube, but when I tried to turn, I slipped. The wave engulfed me, and I started to roll over and over without being able to breathe until I completely ran out of air. I saw the tunnel, the light that precedes cerebral death. At the beginning, a lack of oxygen produces a feeling of pain, but then you reach a point where you relax, perhaps because it increases your carbon dioxide, and in that moment, I came up to the surface, landing on a coral reef. The wave had reached the sand and dissipated. I was really light-headed, but when I took a breath, I snapped back to life. There I realized the importance of knowing your own limits, measuring the risks and not exceeding your capacity. That experience taught me a lot, and has served in my life too, not just in sports. Big achievements are obtained step by step: don't limit your challenges, challenge your limits!" (José Haya)

With his colleague, Professor Tim Young of Shanghai, on the Great Wall of China. "Do not go where the path may lead, go instead where there is no path and leave a trail," Ralph Waldo Emerson. (Author's archive)

In Tibet, where oxygen is thin. "When coming down from the Everest base camp, we stopped to visit the Rongbuk Monastery, which is the one at the highest altitude in the world, 16,700 feet. We had a nice time with a local family. I was stunned by how isolated they are from the world, and their capacity to survive in such extreme conditions." (Daniel López)

Free fall over the Namibian desert. "Life starts when one leaves one's comfort zone. I think leaving your comfort zone is essential in order to evolve in surgery. Learning something new requires enormous sacrifice and effort, but only those doctors who try to innovate and improve are those who survive. As Charles Darwin said, 'it's not the strongest of the species that survives, nor the most intelligent, but the one that best adapts to change.'" (Author's archive)

National Continuing Medical Education Forum on General Thoracic Surgery at Shanghai Pulmonary Hospital, October 21 and 22, 2016. It is held every year and more than five hundred thoracic surgeons participate, among the best in the world. "The first time they invited me to this forum was in 2013, which marked the origin of the Uniportal VATS training that I periodically direct at this center." (Daniel López)

The Asian team asked Doctor González to participate with them in the latest competition between continents held every year at the European Thoracic Surgery Conference. In 2016, it took place in Naples, Italy, and was attended by 1,000 surgeons. "We won decisively," the doctor remarked. The competition consists of hypothetical surgical cases and theoretical questions. There are a series of qualifying rounds between the participating teams and selections (Asia-America-Europe) and "we were the clear winners of the test." (Author's archive)

CPSIA information can be obtained
at www.ICGtesting.com
Printed in the USA
LVHW080146230520
656346LV00004B/184

9 788468 52337